From Recession to Upturn

Related titles from Law Society Publishing:

Financial Services for Solicitors: Law, Practice and Precedents
SIFA (Solicitors Independent Financial Advice), Edited by Ian Muirhead

Guide to Good Practice
The Law Society

Lexcel Practice Excellence Kit, 4th edn
The Law Society with Matthew Moore

Marketing Legal Services: Succeeding in the New Legal Marketplace
David Monk and Alastair Moyes

Practice Management Handbook, 2nd edn
Edited by Peter Scott

Profitability and Law Firm Management, 2nd edn
Andrew Otterburn

Setting Up and Managing a Legal Practice, 3rd edn
Martin Smith

Titles from Law Society Publishing can be ordered from all good bookshops or direct (telephone 0870 850 1422, email **law.society@prolog.uk.com** or visit our online shop at **www.lawsociety.org.uk/bookshop**).

From Recession to Upturn

Financial management and strategy for law firms

Andrew Otterburn and Sarah Wilkinson

The Law Society

ISBN–13: 978–1–85328–794–7

Published in 2009 by the Law Society
113 Chancery Lane, London WC2A 1PL

Typeset by Columns Design Ltd, Reading
Printed by Hobbs the Printers Ltd, Totton, Hants

The paper used for the text pages of this book is FSC certified. FSC (the Forest Stewardship Council) is an international network to promote responsible management of the world's forests.

FSC
Mixed Sources
Product group from well-managed forests and other controlled sources
Cert no. SA-COC-1530
www.fsc.org
© 1996 Forest Stewardship Council

Contents

About the authors

Andrew Otterburn

A chartered accountant and management consultant, Andrew has advised around 250 firms in the UK and Ireland on their management and profitability. His most recent book, *Profitability and Law Firm Management* was published by the Law Society in 2002, with the second edition published in 2007. He is joint author of the annual survey of law firms in Scotland, published by the Law Society of Scotland.

In 2006 he was an adviser to Lord Carter's review of legal aid procurement in England and Wales.

He is a course tutor at the Nottingham Law School, a member of the Executive Committee of the Law Management Section, and a founding member of the Law Consultancy Network.

Sarah Wilkinson

Sarah Wilkinson qualified as a chartered accountant with Touche Ross in London in 1988, having graduated from Durham University in 1985. She was Group Financial Controller at Clifford Chance LLP from 2000 to 2004 and previously worked at Eversheds LLP in London. She is Finance Director for Field Fisher Waterhouse LLP.

Colin FitzPatrick

Colin was a partner in Grant Thornton for 10 years where he specialised in partnerships, mainly solicitors. He was the North East's representative on the firm's National Legal Business Panel, and was on their Business Valuation Panel.

In 1998 Colin established FitzPatrickRoyle as an independent practice, undertaking business advisory and forensic accounting work. The practice has several legal business clients and Colin has undertaken a number of consultancy assignments for them covering partnership structure, mergers and dissolutions.

In 2007 Colin undertook a mergers pilot project as part of Lord Carter's Review of Legal Aid Procurement, which looked at the opportunities for promoting mergers between smaller criminal law firms. He has also lectured for the Law Society and other organisations on various legal business matters and wrote three chapters in the Law Management Section's *Mergers Toolkit* published in 2007.

Howard Hackney

Howard Hackney established his own boutique accountancy practice, Howard Hackney LLP, in 2008 after 25 years as a partner with Grant Thornton.

During his time at Grant Thornton he has had a variety of roles although his 'first love' has always been client service. He has been based in Liverpool and Warrington in the North West of England for most of his career. He joined Grant Thornton in Liverpool in 1974 before moving to London for three years.

In 2002 he won the CBI's national award as 'Best Business Adviser' having been shortlisted in 2001. Howard was co-author of Grant Thornton's 'The credit crunch: a practical guide' and is regular contributor to both the broadcast and print media including 'Ask the Expert' for the *Financial Times* on Saturday. He speaks regularly at seminars and conferences.

Fiona Westwood

Fiona Westwood worked in private practice for 20 years before setting up Westwood Associates in 1994 as a management consultancy specialising in strategic development for professional firms.

She is a founding member of the Law Consultancy Network, a member of the Law Society of Scotland's Standards Working Party and CPD project leader on their Education and Training Review.

Her first book, *Achieving Best Practice* was nominated by McGraw-Hill as their September 2000 Book of the Month. The revised edition of her second book, *Accelerated Best Practice* has recently been published.

Simon Young

A solicitor since 1977, and former managing partner, Simon took the MBA in Legal Practice Management at Nottingham Law School. He has been on the Executive of the Law Management Section of the Law Society since 1999, and since 2001 has represented that Section on the Law Society Council. He chairs the Rules & Ethics group on the representative side of the Society. He is a founding member of the Law Consultancy Network.

He assists law firms with mergers, conversion to LLP status, management and structural matters, and, increasingly, with compliance issues. He has a particular interest in the Legal Services Act, and the business possibilities for law firms in the legislation relating to legal disciplinary practices and alternative business structures.

Simon's solo publications include *Limited Liability Partnerships Handbook* (2nd edition, 2007, Tottell Publishing); the Law Society's *New Partners' Guide to Management*; and the volumes constituting the 'Partnership' title of the *Encyclopaedia of Forms and Precedents*. Joint publications include the *Money Laundering Reporting Officer's Handbook* (LexisNexis); and the Law Society's *Office Procedures Manual*.

Foreword from the Chair of the Law Management Section

I am pleased to have been asked to write the foreword for this important new publication.

The last 12 months have presented finance directors and managing partners with challenges of a kind most had not experienced previously in their professional lifetimes. As Andrew and Sarah say, it is now critical for law firms to stabilise their finances to ensure survival and prepare for future prosperity. Cash has always been king, but perhaps in benign market conditions it is easy for firms to fall into bad financial management habits. No firm can afford to ignore this book's advice. Even in the very best run of law firms, this work still serves a useful purpose as both reminder and checklist.

While surviving the recession is a goal in itself, well-led firms are also planning for a return to prosperity. This work addresses the challenges ahead in the post-Clementi world and steers firms towards developing realistic plans and strategies for the upturn – whenever that may be. Andrew and Sarah's chapters are complemented by others from authors well known in their own particular fields.

One of Andrew's previous works, *Profitability and Law Firm Management*, has become a standard reference tool for those involved in the management of law firms. Andrew and Sarah's work looks set to occupy a similar position, because cash will still be king long after this recession is over.

Nigel Haddon

Chair, Law Management Section, Executive Committee

June 2009

Part 1

The effect of the economic slowdown on firms

Chapter 1

2009 to 2012 – a changing landscape for law firms

The impact on firms so far

Recent months have been tough for most law firms. In times of economic slowdown law firms suffer along with the rest of the economy, and the last year has been a period of major re-adjustment and change. As a partner from a niche commercial firm commented – 'When our clients suffer, we suffer.'

The recession appears to have affected smaller firms first, with many redundancies over the summer and autumn of 2008, and the City feeling the full impact in 2009. A small number of the larger regional and City firms announced staff reductions during 2008, but the main pressure seems to have been felt by them in the early months of 2009.

There are now few firms that have not announced redundancies, or moved staff on to short-time working, and at least two – both volume conveyancing operations – have been put into administration. Firms are now starting to publish accounts that cover the period of decline, and these show the true scale of the problems they face. As always, those with weak finances or business models overly dependent upon just one sector are most at risk. Relatively small declines in fee levels have resulted in significant falls in profits as many overheads, at least in the short term, are fixed. There are higher levels of borrowings and banks have increasingly started to require personal guarantees, or in some cases, debentures on the firm's assets. Most firms make provision for partners' income tax each year, and retain reserves for partners' tax; however not all do, and the position for them will be exacerbated by having to make high income tax payments at a time of both reduced cash collections from clients and falling margins.

The position may well be most difficult for some of the top 100 firms, whose income was substantially dependent on a flow of large deals, who employ large numbers of staff, and who often have high levels of fixed overheads. Ironically High Street firms, whose long-term future is generally regarded as more vulnerable following the Legal Services Act, may find it easier to adjust.

Smaller firms that were highly dependent on property have come under greatest pressure; however, many firms with fewer than, say, 10 partners often have a relatively broad range of income streams from both business and private clients. Approximately 2,500 firms still retain a legal aid contract and in these difficult times they will have been very grateful for the regular monthly payments.

Some of these smaller firms who have made cut-backs and redundancies in the summer and latter part of 2008 appear to be approaching 2009 with greater confidence; indeed by April 2009 a number of firms were reporting increased levels of activity in property related work:

> York did not see the highs that Leeds experienced during the boom, but similarly does not appear to be seeing the same lows now. Our fees are down 7 per cent, but we have made no redundancies, and have just recruited two staff.

> In 2008 we cut our staff levels from around 190 to 150 – we have analysed and analysed and now have a much better understanding of our business. We are in much better control and our plan for this year is to increase profits over last year albeit from a bad year.
>
> Our conveyancing team needs around 40 live matters at any one time to be viable. In January they had just 15 but by April they were flat out with around 70.

It is also interesting to look at firms in Ireland, where the recession started about 18 months ahead of the UK. Whilst conveyancing fees fell considerably, many firms saw income from other work types increase, resulting in overall fees in 2008 not much different from the previous year, in some cases higher.

We may well see a similar pattern in the UK: that firms go through an extremely painful process of staff reductions as they scale back their operations to the new volumes of activity, but then start to move forward again, albeit from a much smaller base.

For larger firms and those more dependent upon property the period of uncertainty will take longer and the contraction to new levels of activity will be more painful, but once again a recovery point will eventually be reached.

The key area – cash

The key area of course in this changing landscape is cash. Profits are important, but for now the emphasis has to be on cash.

Firms that were already overexposed financially at the start of the recession will be the most vulnerable: those with insufficient levels of partner capital, high levels of relatively fixed commitments (rent, leases, fixed annuities, etc.), weak financial controls and a dependence on bank borrowing. In many of these firms the partners will struggle to inject additional capital as they have over-borrowed personally, and have a high level of personal outgoings. A number of these firms will not survive and their weaknesses will overwhelm them. We expect to see an increase in merger activity, some from positions of weakness rather than strength.

These firms will be most vulnerable, but few firms are naturally good at managing cash. In smaller firms some partners still regard the cashier's office as a highly convenient ATM; in firms of all sizes partners and fee earners are not good at quoting for work, billing and chasing payment. They dislike the latter more than anything and in the current climate are especially nervous of upsetting clients.

Firms have to become excellent at these areas – billing, chasing debts and cash management, and these are the areas where much of this book concentrates.

A two-stage process – stabilise the business then prepare for the upturn

It is very easy to feel panicked in these days of 24-hour news coverage; however, as already indicated, the situation may well not be as bleak for many firms as might appear at first glance. Most firms would benefit from adopting a two-stage process to the management of their business over the coming year:

1. Stabilise the firm's finances and establish strong levels of financial management – as discussed in Part 2;

2. Revise and update your firm's long-term strategy – much has changed and is continuing to change. In order to be a player in five years' time, indeed in order to still be around, you will need to update your plans and you will need to think long-term. This is developed in Part 3.

The wider landscape

Before the onset of the recession the legal profession was already facing major change as a result of the Legal Services Act 2007. These challenges remain – they may well have changed as result of the recession; in particular prospective entrants may well not find it as easy to raise funds. However, the basic changes, threats and opportunities remain.

Perhaps the one good thing to be said of the recession is that many smaller firms have now experienced the reductions in conveyancing volumes that were likely to result from the Act, as work that had traditionally flowed to them went instead to the volume processors. It is perhaps ironic that it was two of these high volume operations, overly dependent upon property, which were the first to go into administration.

So, as part of the planning process, firms need to look ahead to what the wider legal landscape might look like as we emerge from of the recession. What might be the impact of the Legal Services Act?

The one thing firms can be certain of is that the world will be more competitive and that the winners will be those with effective management. They will need good people, with excellent leadership skills; they will need to provide high standards of client service; they will need clear positions in the market – but they will all need to be well-run businesses. They will need sound and effective financial management.

Chapter 2

Firms in trouble

As already indicated two high profile administrations of law firms occurred early in 2009 and the banks are closely monitoring many others. Unfortunately there will be a number of firms that do not survive the recession and the implications for their partners will be significant.

As always the key is to try to be ahead of the situation and take action or obtain advice at an early stage. You also need to keep your bank informed of what is happening. Even if everything is fine, make sure you keep talking to your bank.

The warning signs[1]

Warning signs are difficult to interpret since the majority of firms and practitioners who have serious financial problems end up in that situation as the result of an aggregation of different (and perhaps wholly unrelated) events or causes. The effect is cumulative. Each early warning sign, taken on its own, can probably be explained and dealt with very easily and most practitioners do just that – entertaining is cut back a little; conferences and subscriptions are cancelled. As a last measure, drawings are reduced or linked to monthly cash collection per partner or department. There are many variations on these cost-cutting measures.

If a firm is in serious financial difficulties, it is not enough simply to cut back on expenditure here or there. It is of prime and vital importance that the root cause or causes of the problem should be identified and treated. The identification and treatment process is often painful and, understandably, one which most people will seek to avoid. However, the sad fact is that the longer the problem is avoided, the more difficult the solution.

Look at the following eight questions. Answer them honestly and consider the results:

- Do you wake up at 4am and have difficulty going back to sleep, the rest of the night spent tossing and turning and thinking about your problems?
- Does your stomach churn when the phone rings at about 11am and you hear that it is the bank who wants to speak to you?
- Do you dread looking at letters in the post marked 'private and confidential' which are addressed to you?
- Do you almost pray for each day to end?
- Have you noticed that your appetite is not as good as it was in the past?
- Are you drinking more heavily than normal?
- Have you lost all interest in something that you used to enjoy as a leisure pastime?
- Have the bags under your eyes become bigger?

1 This section is based on a contribution to *Cash Flow and Improved Financial Management* (Law Society, 1998) by Cormac Smith.

If you have answered yes to more than about three of these questions, it is likely that the stress you are under is at, or is approaching, a highly debilitating level. If this has arisen as a result of financial problems, it is of vital importance that you seek help immediately.

Another way to deal with the questions is to look at the difference between the answers you give privately to yourself and the answers you would give if asked those questions by a close friend. If there is a noticeable gap between the two, there is a real danger that you know there is a problem and are avoiding facing up to it. That merely adds to the seriousness of the problem and the need to seek help.

Talk to someone as soon as possible

It can be very difficult to find the courage to talk to someone. Perhaps a starting point in overcoming your reticence is the realisation that your problems are not unique. Many legal aid solicitors will be facing similar issues. A firm or a lawyer is not alone in having financial problems and there is no disgrace or shame in it.

The other problem is to whom to speak. This is very difficult since, although financial problems are, in one sense, a great leveller, the particular type of problems that a solicitor faces need specialist understanding and that understanding can best and (often) only come from another member of the profession.

You probably will feel shy of speaking to the Law Society, and your bank will probably not be helpful. Your accountant will doubtless be sympathetic, but may not understand what has caused the problems and how to cure them – and this is even more the case if he or she has been your accountant for some time.

The specialist insolvency members of the Solicitors' Assistance Scheme (**www.thesas.org.uk**) are ideally placed to assist. They are neither judgemental nor condescending and have experience dealing with these issues.[2]

Whoever you talk to, the most important thing must be that they help you through the difficulties so that you can carry on practising free of stress and find an effective remedy.

Taking action before it is too late – Howard Hackney[3]

'Turnover is vanity, profits are sanity and cash is reality' goes the old saying and never is it more true than for firms facing financial difficulties. While it is rare that a focus on turnover is the key to firms facing imminent difficulties, whether to focus on profit or cash will depend on where the practice is in the scale of difficulties. In the very short term a business fails through lack of cash while in the medium term it is generally through the lack of profits.

Management 'with clout'

Recognition and acceptance of the problem is probably the first and most important hurdle to overcome, as in many cases the majority of partners may not be aware of the problems and will

2 For practical and confidential guidance on practice or personal issues call the Solicitors' Assistance Scheme on 0207 117 8811.

3 Howard Hackney is the Principal of Howard Hackney LLP.

not therefore be focusing as a team on what really matters. Even when they do realise the scale and depth of the problem there is then the issue of how to put it right. It is not unknown for a practice to recognise the problem but then not know what to do and as a result the partners end up meeting weekly without really addressing the key issues or taking any action. This really is the crisis of management that so often occurs and has brought the firm to the financial position it currently faces. If this is the case the first thing to do is to ensure that the partners appoint a management team 'with clout' who can take the difficult decisions necessary in a decisive fashion without endless debate and intellectual discussion until the position is irretrievable, and who will be supported by the partners.

'It's easy isn't it?'

Once the management team is in place the solution is easy – isn't it?

- Reduce costs.
- Increase income.
- Reduce lock-up.

If only it were that easy! Each of these areas will produce significant management challenges and require clarity of thinking as to what the key actions are as each action taken will have its positive and negative aspects. This requires information on the KPIs (see Chapter 5) but with a clear focus on which are the important ones and in what order of priority. In comparison with the budget these are likely to be daily cash received, fees billed, chargeable hours and new instructions received. The budget will have been set in advance using the simple 'office model' showing evaluated achievable chargeable hours per fee earner against forecast fee income. This can then be used to determine the 'right size' of the practice.

Cost reduction

Cost reduction is the quickest and easiest area to consider but bear in mind that the largest cost for any practice is its partners and staff. Whilst cutting staff will impact in the longer term on fee income, cutting quickly and more deeply than is on the face of it necessary is probably the best approach. It gets the negative impact on overall morale out of the way early on and in spite of the costs of redundancy will produce an immediate saving in cash outflow. Cutting partners may be part of this process and hence the need for partner support at the outset. However unpleasant cutting partners and staff may be, management must keep their sights firmly on the longer term benefit to the majority of partners and staff.

Increasing income

This is more of a medium-term measure as income cannot always be generated that quickly once it has already declined. However, partners and staff should be targeted on increasing income and the usual easiest source of this is through cross-referrals from other departments and from existing clients. The mindset of all fee earners becomes far more focused when the issue is one of survival rather than just the level of bonus. Where practices have a volume operation and work comes from referral fees there is often significant fee income that can be 'bought' in. Given the length of time taken to convert such work it is almost certainly not a strategy to adopt to increase fee income and indeed reducing volumes of such work will actually increase cash inflow.

Reducing lock-up and controlling cash

This is probably the weakest area of financial management in any practice and one that can produce the biggest gains. The techniques mentioned in Part 2 should be employed but one of the most effective (and draconian) is to link partners' drawings to cash collected. There will always be the arguments about differing departments' lock-up profile and whether to make it individual, department or firm specific and the negative impact it will have on clients, but this is where strong management can cut through those arguments and make a real and significant difference. Relentless cash management on a day by day and week by week basis will be vital for practices that are at the most critical stage and weekly cash flow forecasts will need to be produced and payments to suppliers delayed. Tax has historically been a liability that has been a problem but in this recession HMRC, with government backing, is actually being very helpful in agreeing deferral of liabilities so do not be afraid to approach them.

Managing your banking relationship is also very important. Keeping your bank manager fully informed and part of your team is still good advice but in this recession and against the well-publicised problems with the banks, all due care must be taken in when and how to approach your bank.

Restrictions in drawings will never be welcome but as owners of the business who take the risks and rewards you must always make this high on the list of options – especially as borrowing limits are approached.

If matters become particularly critical, advice should be taken from a Licensed Insolvency Practitioner (IP) and partners should be alive to their personal financial exposure. They should take steps to mitigate that exposure but under the guidance of the IP. They must not prejudice the interests of creditors while not 'throwing good money after bad'.

Dealing with your bank

It is clearly important that in the current economic climate your bank is kept fully informed of how your firm is doing – make sure it knows what is happening, and in particular avoid surprises.

You need to be aware that banks tend to have several rules of thumb regarding lending to professional services firms and it might be worthwhile keeping these in mind. Here are some of the commonly used benchmarks:

- Partner capital should be greater than bank debt. Banks don't like to lend law firms more capital than that contributed by the partners.
- The bank would compare the overdraft – which would normally be provided to fund working capital – to their estimate of recoverable working capital – perhaps 50 per cent of debtors and 30 per cent of work in progress (WIP).
- For larger firms, 10 per cent of fee income is a benchmark used by some banks when looking at overdraft levels.
- A year's money. In a well-run larger law firm, the bank might expect the profit available for distribution to the partners to exceed total partners' funds at the balance sheet date. If partners' funds exceed profits the implication is that margins may be poor and/or working capital is sluggish. But if profits are greater than partners' funds it implies good margins and/or excessive debt or an over-rapid pay-out of profits.

By way of example, if the profit generated and appropriated to partners for the current year is £300,000, then the working capital of the firm should be turning over sufficiently well to enable all of the profit and any associated tax due to be paid out by the end of the following year. Even if the partners' current accounts include a further £150,000 of retained tax reserves and undrawn profits by the balance sheet date, the cash flows should be sufficiently healthy to permit these to be paid out by the end of the next financial year. This might not be possible owing to the rapid growth of the firm, or the profile of its cases; however for most firms it should be possible and this can be a useful benchmark.

Two bankers who specialise in the sector give their views below.

Keeping the bank informed – what your bank will expect from you – Mike Holloway[4]

Your bank will require a number of things from you, including a comprehensive 'non-financial' business plan. This should include:

- A realistic assessment of the marketplace in which the business operates.
- Well thought-out, high level and operational strategies covering:
  - In which markets will the firm operate and how it can achieve a sustainable competitive advantage.
  - How the firm will compete in those markets – the actions the partners/stakeholders are going to take in order to deliver their services. There needs to be a full consideration of key competitors and their impact on achieving the high level strategy.
  - The enabling actions necessary to give effect to the operational strategies including marketing, IT, finance and human resources.
- A well-balanced management structure – consider taking advantage where appropriate of the alternative business structures (ABSs) provisions of the Legal Services Act 2007 to bring in top quality professional management to deliver one or more of the key strategies.
- A clear demonstration of a business model appropriate to the strategies and incorporating delivery to market, the deployment of appropriate human resources, the optimal use of IT and an understanding of the key performance criteria necessary to deliver the strategies.
- Strong financial management:
  - Comprehensive, integrated financial budgets together with written assumptions, evidencing ability to repay debt whilst meeting the remuneration expectations of the stakeholders.
  - Clear, accurate and timely management information which summarises performance versus budget in key areas such as income, expenditure and profit and confirmation of adherence to any agreed performance criteria.
  - Regular review of key areas of cost and a willingness to take decisive action where necessary to preserve profitability.
  - Emphasis on maximising cash flow through strong working capital management – effective billing of WIP and collection of outstanding bills – and through managing the remuneration expectations of the partners where necessary.

4 Mike Holloway is an Associate Director in the Professional Practices Group at the Royal Bank of Scotland.

- A clear purpose to funding with repayment structured over a period appropriate to that purpose and a level of headroom to cover unforeseen circumstances.
- Details of relative levels of partner (or other external) capital and debt appropriate to the business mix of the firm. The relationship between capital and debt should be kept under regular review and adjusted where necessary to reflect changes in the financial circumstances of the business – including:
  - Changes in the business mix, for example to areas of practice which are more cash consuming.
  - Changes in the equity partnership, especially the exit of senior partners with large amounts of capital.
  - Investment in fixed assets such as property or substantial IT projects.

Your bank will require regular contact with honest and open discussion around the key issues and above all ... no nasty surprises!

Existing problems in sharper focus – getting the basics right – Chris Marston[5]

It has never been more important to get the basics right, and firms that can organise their businesses to be profitable and resilient in challenging conditions will be set to fly when the market improves. I have seen some very practical ways of generating improvements in this area, such as:

- Regular peer oversight, whereby a fee earner from another department challenges the WIP, disbursement and debtor figures of a colleague in another discipline and is subject to similar scrutiny himself.
- 'Billing days' throughout the year, where on a set day the whole firm, or a department at a time, clears the appointments diary and sets aside time to raise bills. Even now we see firms raising 25 per cent of annual billing in month 12! Among some fee earners there is a mentality of 'keeping something up my sleeve', but this is surely a luxury few can afford. The same principle can be applied to debtor collection, particularly those stubborn cases where the bill remains outstanding because of a dispute on a small part of the bill. Lawyers by inclination can be tempted to argue points of fine detail – that's why we use them – but the bigger picture is to get paid, and if a deal has to be struck or a compromise reached, then almost always that will be the right answer.

There are a number of key differences from the recession of the late 1980s and early 1990s. First, interest rates are low rather than being in double figures. Second, the Chancellor this time has different concerns. Inflation is falling rather than rising. A credit bubble has burst and markets around the world are adjusting painfully.

For many businesses, a low base rate is good news. Not so for solicitors, whose borrowing costs have tended to be a minor consideration compared to their ability to generate revenue from client monies.

Fortunately most firms are reacting more quickly and decisively to deteriorating economic conditions than they did last time. Many managing partners remember the longer term cost of delaying hard decisions, and have been determined to act swiftly this time around.

5 Chris Marston is Head of Solicitors Banking at Lloyds TSB Bank plc.

More importantly, this recession coincides with a period of sweeping change in the legal profession of quite unprecedented scale, and growing numbers of mergers and retirements demonstrate that the consolidation that has been underway for some time is gathering pace.

There is a need to ensure a matching of liabilities so that the overdraft is used for what it was designed for, i.e. working capital.

Perhaps motivated by the reduction of credit availability, some law firms are now considering other facets of the financing mix, in particular the capital within the business. This has started at the top, with Clifford Chance announcing a £40 million cash call from its 400 partners in January 2009, and the concept is starting to filter through to smaller firms. Many firms are insufficiently capitalised, and the still-prevalent partnership business model has done nothing to encourage the retention of capital in law firms. Partners who have been able to take significant drawings over the past several years are now considering putting some cash back in. Where they have the assets but lack the liquidity to achieve this, banks will consider partner equity loans.

In the interests of balance I should say that some law firms are doing remarkably well at the moment – it all depends upon the business mix and there's no doubt that strong management and having some counter-cyclical work in the portfolio helps.

For most solicitors' practices, however, it has never been more important to maintain an open and honest dialogue with their bankers. Banks want to help customers to get through this recession and emerge from it stronger than before.

Part 2

Effective financial management to stabilise the business

Chapter 3

Stabilising the business – cash and profitability

Most firms have so far responded to the effects of the recession by making redundancies and cutting back on expenditure they perceive as unnecessary. In many cases it has been fairly clear which departments or areas of work were losing money, and it was often equally clear which partners and staff should go. For most it has been a painful and extremely difficult period.

Whilst most firms will undoubtedly need to scale back their operations, as already highlighted, the area they actually need to focus on first is cash. Perversely, redundancies may actually exacerbate a firm's short-term cash position, so whilst they need to be on your agenda they should not necessarily be at the top.

Improving cash – the initial areas to look at

If you want to improve your cash position the first area to tackle is working capital management because most firms in the UK still have huge amounts of money locked up in work in progress, debtors and disbursements. If you need to actually improve cash flow, improvements in these areas are likely to have the most immediate impact. Much of this first section is devoted to this key area.

At the same time you should look at partner drawings and partner capital. It will be painful but necessary:

- You need to adjust partner drawings to the lower levels of profits you are now forecasting. In particular you need to ensure that drawings do not exceed the firm's cash profits, as part of your firm's profits will represent movements in both work in progress and debtors. Partners normally regard any changes to their drawings as the last measure to look at, whereas it should really be one of the first.
- Allied to drawings is the overall level of capital the partners have invested in the firm. Figure 3.1 suggests that median partner capital in firms in 2008 was approximately £133,000. This represents total partner capital – both current and fixed capital – and is based on the respondents to the 2008 Financial Benchmarking Survey undertaken by the Law Management Section (LMS).[1] As a matter of interest, in the 2008 Law Society of Scotland Benchmarking Survey[2] median partner capital was £88,000. In both surveys some firms have quite high levels of partner capital; however, others have low levels. An urgent question to consider is

1 Based upon returns from 108 member firms, the survey is not necessarily representative of the profession as a whole, but provides an indication of the performance of firms. Classification is by *total* number of partners. It should be noted that in the report published by the LMS the classification was based on number of equity partners only. We have only showed the median for 25-plus partner firms, due to the small number of participants.

2 *Law Society of Scotland: Benchmarks and the Cost of Time*. This survey, based on a large sample, is representative of firms in Scotland.

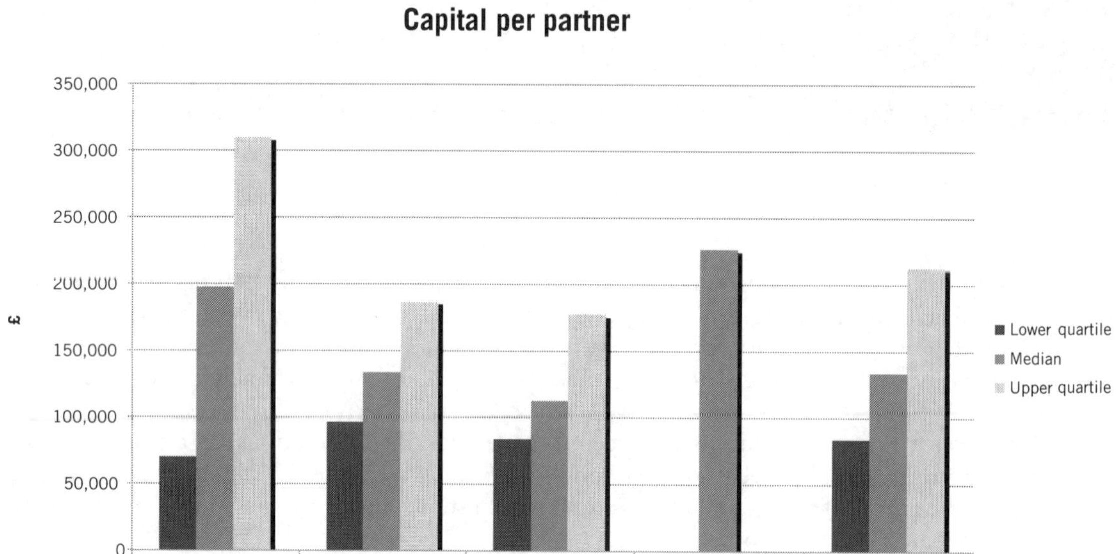

	2-4	5-10	11-25	25+	All
Lower quartile	70,611	96,790	83,906		83,375
Median	198,118	133,333	112,526	225,850	133,333
Upper quartile	309,744	185,985	177,434		212,056

Figure 3.1 Capital per partner (LMS Benchmarking Survey 2008)

whether partners' capital in your firm is sufficient? If not, a very quick way of improving the firm's cash position is an injection of additional capital from the partners. In particular you may need to increase partner capital if it is less than your firm's bank borrowings, as banks will often, at the very least, require parity in funding.

- Because it is important to maintain the confidence of your bank it is important that partners do not overdraw their current accounts at the present time, and they should certainly not overdraw their total capital without the advance agreement of your bank. Unfortunately, because partners are often slow to adjust the level of their drawings, this may well happen in many firm's accounts, unless the partners take action before the year-end to remedy the situation. This will not necessarily be easy but will generally need to be done – unless you have the agreement of your bank.

For most firms the two times of the year when cash is under greatest strain are when partner income tax has to be paid in January and July. For some firms these times will coincide with VAT quarters and rent payments, and for a few the accumulation will push them into cash flow difficulties. To minimise the risk, areas to consider include:

- retaining part of the profits within the firm to cover partner income tax;
- transferring an amount each month into a separate deposit account in respect of partner tax, so you have the money already put to one side;
- transferring an amount each month in respect of VAT so once again you have the money put to one side each quarter.

Having first reviewed your firm's working capital, drawings and partner capital, move on to look at overheads and salaries.

Overheads

As many partners know, most overheads are basically fixed – at least in the short term. It is possible to squeeze savings from overheads, and certainly many firms have found that over the last year they have been able to save some money; however, the overall potential is limited.

It can be useful to group overheads into three categories, those that are:

- fixed or relatively fixed, e.g. rent, business tax, depreciation;
- variable but necessary, e.g. telephones, stationery, insurance; or
- variable but discretionary, e.g. marketing, training, IT, external advice.

Those in the latter group are frequently the first to be cut in an economic slowdown yet they are arguably items that should be left alone or perhaps even increased. Items in the latter group are in effect investment areas and by cutting these areas firms risk damage in the longer term. Even the best firms rarely spend more than 1 or 2 per cent of fees each on marketing and training, so the amounts saved are modest compared to the longer term harm.

The first two groups comprise the bulk of non-salary overheads. Many, such as rent, business tax and depreciation are fixed, at least in the short term. Fixed overheads might amount to 10 per cent of fees, possibly more. The major part of non-salary overheads for most firms is therefore in the second group – variable but necessary.

This is an area where it can be useful to spend some time. Matters to consider include:

- *Cost reduction* – in the past most firms have not spent much time negotiating prices from their suppliers, but by obtaining quotes and actively seeking value for money it may be possible to save 10 per cent, perhaps more. Start with the items you spend most on and seek to negotiate better prices – A4 paper, envelopes, notepads, counsel pads, insurance, telephones, accountancy, etc. If the local supplier appears expensive you might get a better deal on the internet. Adopt a policy to: never accept the first price quoted; never sacrifice quality for price; and always get at least three competitive quotes for any major purchase.
- *Outsourcing of services* – perhaps IT and HR support to specialist companies, or typing to lower cost countries, simultaneously taking advantage of different time zones.
- *Review working methods* – to eliminate wasteful processes and working methods – in particular amongst fee earners. This would include examining the use of IT within the firm, levels of fee earner, use of support staff and ways of reducing unit cost.

When assessing whether your firm's overheads are reasonable it is useful to look at:

- Overheads as a percentage of fees – typically this is around 30 per cent. Generally the overheads figure as shown in the accounts needs to be adjusted for:
  - notional rent, where the partners own their offices and the firm does not actually pay them any rent – which is the case in many smaller firms;
  - notional interest on partner capital to reflect the 'real' cost of providing finance to the firm.

Figures 3.2 and 3.3 illustrate that on average non-salary overheads represent around 31 per cent of fees. Figure 3.4 shows that median overheads per fee earner are £34,000.

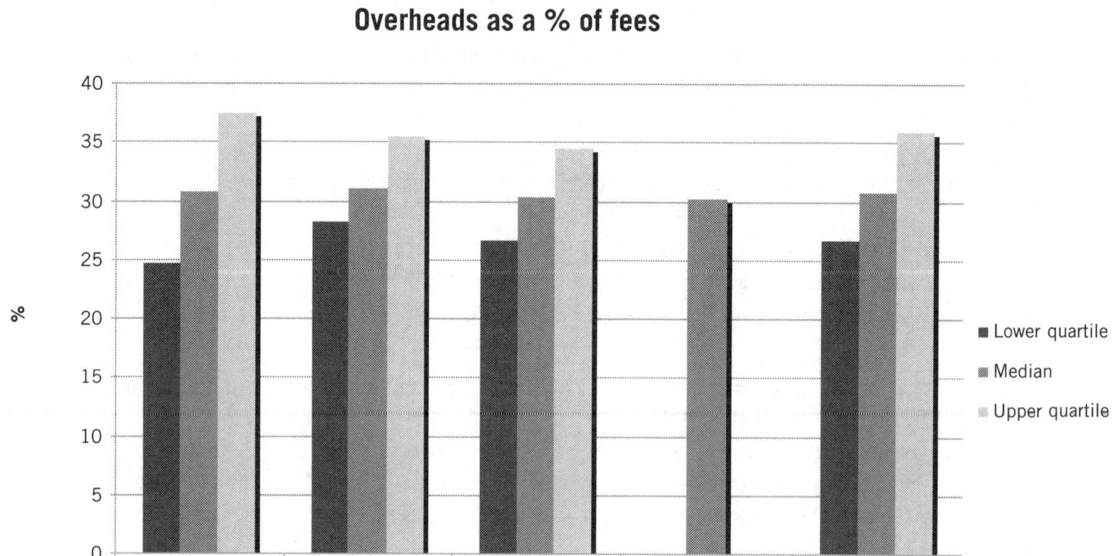

	2–4	5–10	11–25	25+	All
Lower quartile	25	28	27		27
Median	31	31	30	30	31
Upper quartile	37	36	35		36

Figure 3.2 Non-salary overheads as a percentage of fees

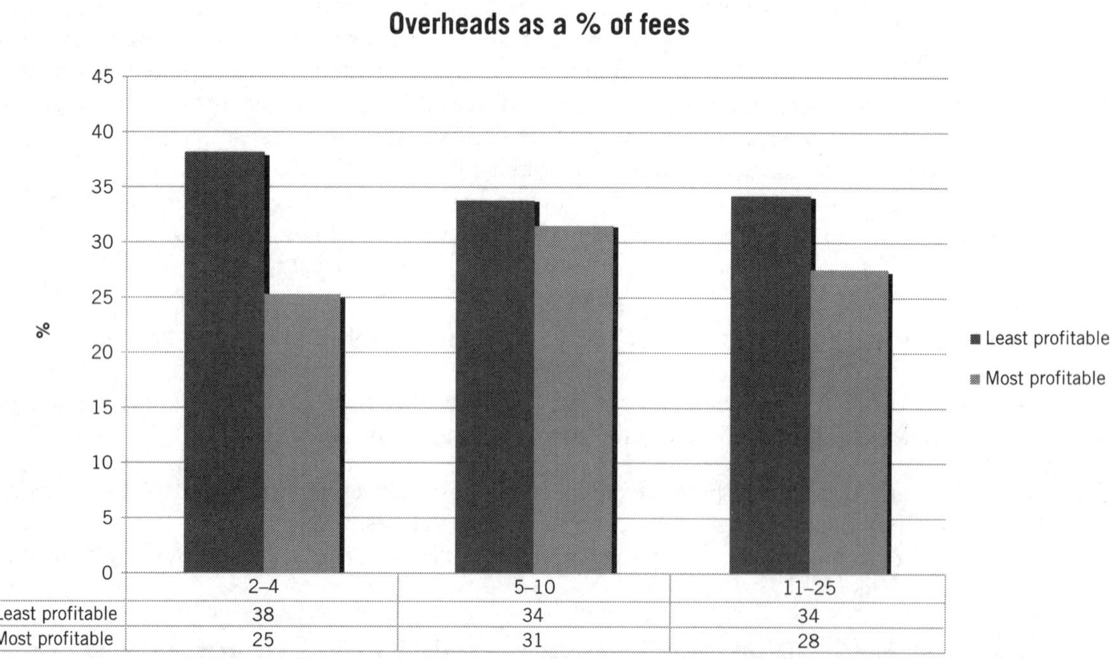

	2–4	5–10	11–25
Least profitable	38	34	34
Most profitable	25	31	28

Figure 3.3 Non-salary overheads as a percentage of fees (highest and lowest)

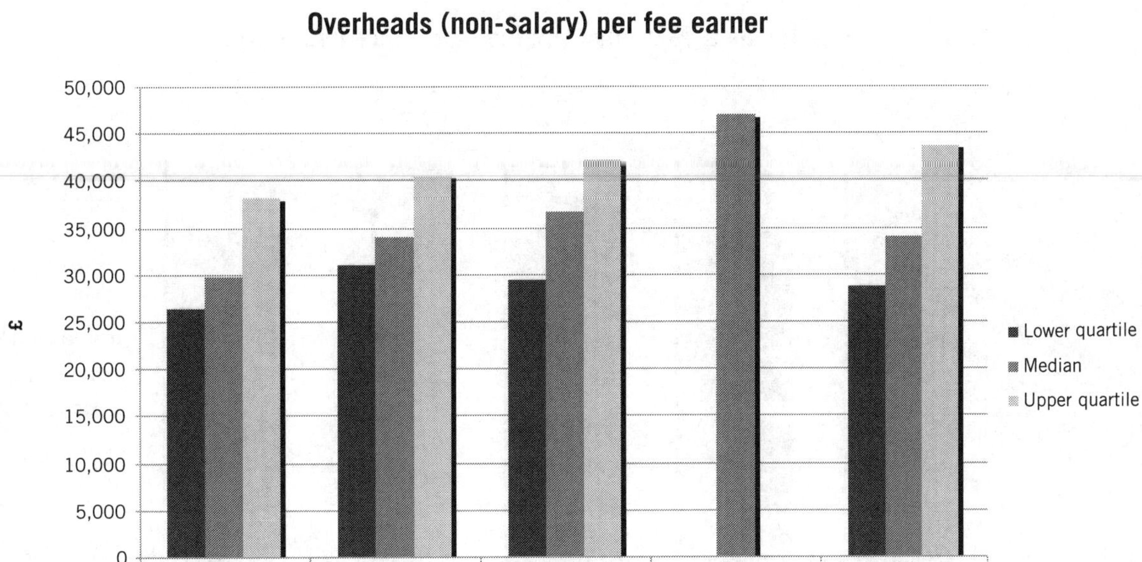

	2–4	5–10	11–25	25+	All
Lower quartile	26,391	30,963	29,497		28,743
Median	29,714	34,055	36,782	47,020	34,055
Upper quartile	38,209	40,346	42,202		43,681

Figure 3.4 Non-salary overheads per fee earner

Salaries and gross margin

Traditionally partners tended to focus purely on the net profit percentage, with 30 per cent often being considered a good benchmark for all but the largest firms, for which a larger profit percentage has been the norm in recent years; however, most firms have now moved beyond this and instead focus on areas such as gross margin.

Gross margin is defined as fees less salaries (and sometimes overheads that are specific to a department). 'Salaries' needs to include a notional salary in respect of each equity partner. Gross margin can be monitored at two levels:

- firm-wide; and
- department or team.

Prior to the recession, firm-wide gross margins were typically 35 per cent. Salaries were around 65 per cent of fees, with departmental salaries accounting for approximately 55 per cent and central support staff around 10 per cent of fees. Departmental or team gross margin was typically therefore around 45 per cent of fees.

Figures 3.5 and 3.6 illustrate overall salaries by size of firm.

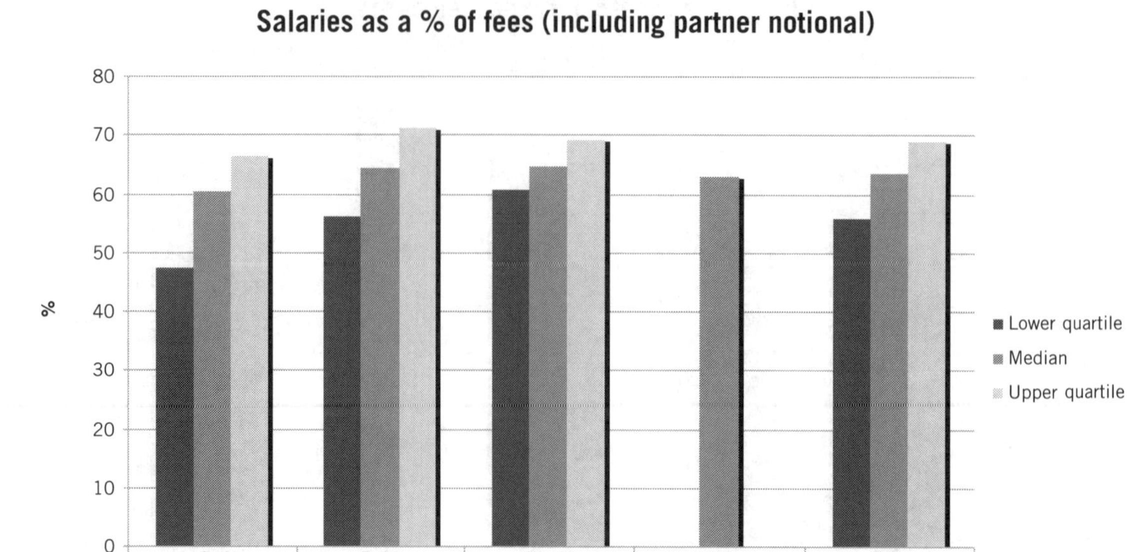

	2–4	5–10	11–25	25+	All
Lower quartile	47	56	61		56
Median	60	64	65	63	64
Upper quartile	66	71	69		69

Figure 3.5 Salaries as a percentage of fees (including partner notional)

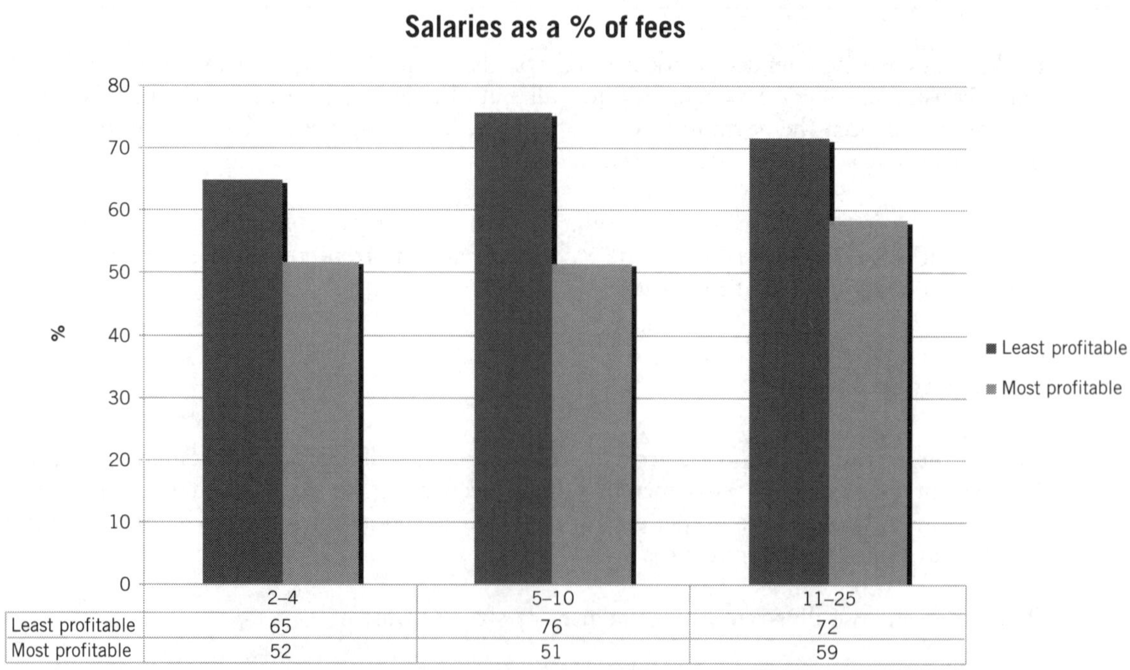

	2–4	5–10	11–25
Least profitable	65	76	72
Most profitable	52	51	59

Figure 3.6 Salaries as a percentage of fees (highest and lowest)

When assessing the performance of fee earners it is necessary to factor in a notional salary in respect of the equity partners. In these charts we have taken the average salary of the highest paid employed fee earner in each size group and added 10 per cent. This resulted in notional salaries of £50,000, £82,000, £96,000 and £125,000 for the four size groups.

The net margin, after having allowed for notional partner salaries, rent and interest on partner capital, may be as low as 5 per cent. This is the 'true' net margin of a law firm and is the equivalent of the margin that would exist in a company. The frequently quoted 30 per cent levels are before these items and can therefore be misleading.

With the recession, all of these benchmarks will have deteriorated, but it will be very useful to keep in mind what had been achieved previously, as these figures will provide good goals for firms to work towards as the economy slowly starts to recover.

Gearing or leverage

Gearing is a key figure to be aware of when considering the longer term development of your firm, as the most profitable firms tend to have higher levels of gearing.

Figure 3.7 indicates that the firms had median gearing of 4.2; however, amongst the most profitable in Figure 3.8 – those achieving profits above the upper quartile – gearing was on average around five fee earners in addition to each equity partner.

Gearing is traditionally measured by reference to the headcount of the non-equity partner fee earners compared to that of the equity partners. An alternative could be to measure gearing by reference to the chargeable hours recorded by these two groups. Ideally the non-partner fee earners should have higher chargeable hours than the partners, owing to the client development and management roles of the latter.

Average cost per hour

The final important figure to highlight at this point is the actual average cost of your fee earner's time. Calculated very easily by taking your total cost base – salaries (including partner notional salaries) plus overheads (including notional rent and interest if appropriate) – and dividing it by your capacity, which is normally expressed in hours.

The average from the LMS survey was a relatively high £110 but the average amongst large crime firms for example was £52, with a quarter under £45. What might the average cost per hour amongst new market entrants be and what might their average cost per fee earner be?

These are figures you need to know for your own firms. (For more guidance see Chapter 14 in Otterburn, A. (2007) *Profitability and Law Firm Management*, 2nd edition, Law Society Publishing.)

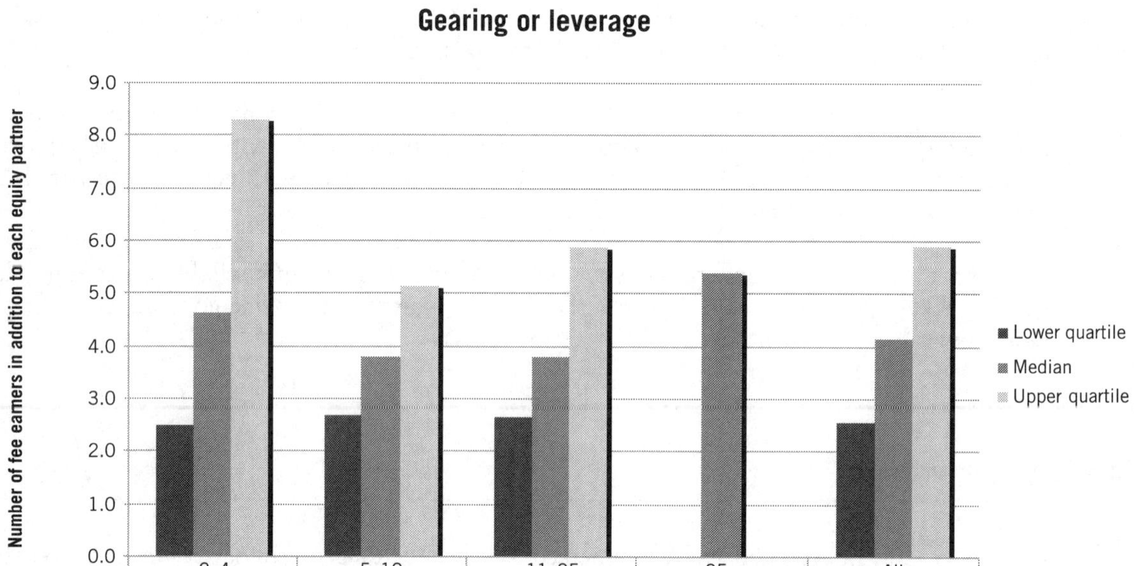

	2–4	5–10	11–25	25+	All
Lower quartile	2.5	2.7	2.7		2.6
Median	4.6	3.8	3.8	5.4	4.2
Upper quartile	8.3	5.2	5.9		5.9

Figure 3.7 Gearing

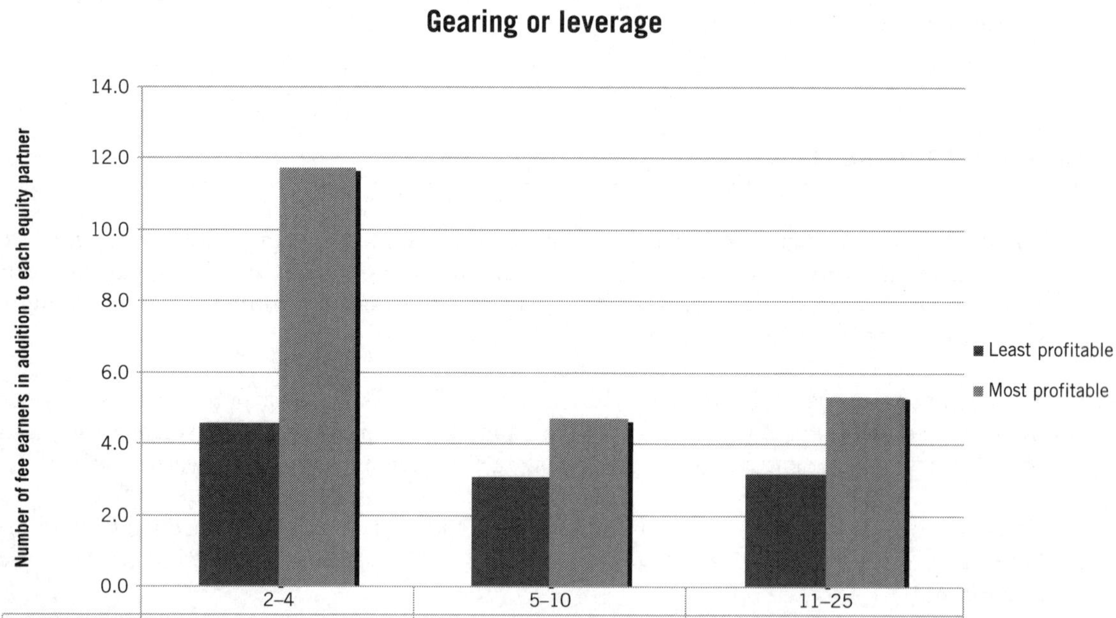

	2–4	5–10	11–25
Least profitable	4.6	3.1	3.2
Most profitable	11.8	4.7	5.3

Figure 3.8 Gearing (highest and lowest)

Case study

High Street, general practice

How many partners does your firm have?	11
How many fee earners (including partners, paralegals and trainees) does your firm have?	45
What is your position in the firm?	Managing partner
Who is responsible for financial management?	Finance partner and managing partner
Could you indicate what action your firm has had to take so far in dealing with the recession?	Reduction in salary costs through combination of natural wastage (i.e. not replacing leavers), redundancy of predominantly support staff (property secretaries and a couple of paralegals – approximately 8 FTEs) and reduced hours to 4-day week for property fee earners.
Do you have any particular suggestions as to things that have worked in helping your firm adjust?	Act early. Our taking action with support staff in the early summer of 2008 certainly helped. Keep working to drive the firm forward – we have proceeded with IT developments and an office relocation, which has helped to keep the firm's profile high. We were also anxious to keep our fee earner team (in property) intact. We have invested much in them and are reluctant to incur substantial recruitment costs when the market recovers, so have tried to concentrate on support staff cuts.
Were there any ideas that have not worked?	We did introduce a new fee earner bonus scheme in early 2008 which has not made a great deal of difference to billing performance.
Do you have any suggestions for managing debtors and WIP?	Regular interim billing. Costs up front, or a payment on account when possible. Strict discipline re disbursements. Discussing ability to pay at an early stage. Review WIP throughout year.
Do you have any suggestions for engaging partners and fee earners and getting them take action to reduce the amounts tied up in working capital?	Monthly credit control reports to partners. Attendance of credit controller at departmental meetings. Keep repeating the same messages! Emphasise that personal responsibility for financial management is part of the job.
What are the main problem areas you face in making progress?	Some fee earners and partners who don't consider financial management to be part of the job. The decline in property work. People 'waiting' for work to come in rather than trying to do something about it. Clients (even those unaffected by the recession) are trying to take longer to pay.
What are the main figures you now look at each month to monitor the financial health of the business?	• P&L • Fee earner billing against budget • Fee earner time recording against budget • WIP • Cash received/bank borrowing • File opening by department

For how long do you expect the current recession to last, specifically in terms of the legal sector rather than the economy at large?	Early 2010?
Who in your firm is responsible for managing:	
(a) utilisation and fee earner payroll costs;	(a) Practice manager/managing partner/accounts manager
(b) leverage and secretarial to fee earner and support staff to fee earner ratios;	(b) Practice manager/managing partner
(c) support staff payroll costs;	(c) Practice manager/managing partner
(d) non-payroll overheads.	(d) Practice manager/managing partner
Any other tips?	Cash is king! Keep watching cash flows and be aware that time must be allowed for any discussions with/decisions by banks.

Chapter 4

Making sure everyone understands the figures

Understanding LLP and partnership accounts

Over the last two or three years the number of firms converting from partnership to LLP has increased and an acceleration seems to have taken place in the latter part of 2008. One of the benefits of an LLP is that the annual accounts follow a more structured format and that, depending on the size of the firm, the figures are subjected to an audit. This is a huge improvement as the layout and detailed information shown in a set of partnership accounts varied widely and very much depended on the approach followed by the accountants concerned. It is now much easier, for example for banks, to compare and interpret the accounts of different firms, as they are prepared in a more consistent way.

Unfortunately, as well as being more structured, LLP accounts are also often more complicated and the language and terms used more technical. They are often difficult to understand by anyone other than accountants. Solicitors can feel daunted by numbers and this added complexity does not help their understanding.

The situation has been aggravated by changes in how the figures themselves are calculated and changes to the basis upon which the accounts have been prepared. Most of these changes have been designed to make the accounts more meaningful but they often seem to have the opposite effect. The most recent change in accounting standards, UITF[1] 40, is perhaps the most obvious example.

Impact of a different accounting basis on your annual accounts

Over the years a number of changes have taken place in the underlying basis that accountants use to prepare partnership accounts. These changes have generally been introduced in order to make the accounts more meaningful and in many ways they have been successful in that objective. By including debtors first and then work in progress they have sought to show the 'real' income and profitability of a firm and to present a realistic balance sheet. As the economy has slowed, however, these more sophisticated ways of preparing accounts almost seem to have the opposite effect of making it more difficult to understand a firm's finances and in particular its cash position.

Thirty years ago all firms prepared their accounts on what was called the 'cash basis'. Most clubs and societies still prepare their accounts on a cash basis today and, literally, the accounts simply show the receipts and payments that have taken place. Tables 4.1 to 4.9 illustrate this with a simple example below.

1 Accounting Standards Board – UITF – Urgent Issues Task Force.

Let us assume a firm starts trading and that in its first year it achieves fees of £550,000 of which £400,000 were paid in the year. It paid out expenses (salaries and overheads) of £450,000. The two partners injected capital of £15,000 each at the start of the year and negotiated an overdraft of £20,000. They took no drawings, waiting to see what the position was at the end of the year. At the end of the year they were at their overdraft limit of £20,000. Tables 4.1 and 4.2 illustrate their position on a *cash* basis:

Table 4.1 Profit and loss account

£'000	Cash basis
Income	400
Expenses	450
Profit/loss	–50

Table 4.2 Balance sheet

£'000	Cash basis
Bank	–20
	–20
Capital	
Capital introduced	30
Profit/loss	–50
	–20

This very simple basis of accounting is what most firms in the UK used 30 years ago. It is what US firms use today. The position was quite straightforward – the firm had made a loss and had borrowings of £20,000 – there was no scope for any drawings.

Whilst easy to understand, this very simple way of producing accounts was criticised as not really showing the true financial health of the firm – HM Revenue and Customs also considered it understated profits – and therefore deferred tax payments! It was argued that income billed but not paid should be brought into account and similarly firms should allow for expenses incurred but not actually paid out by the year-end. The balance sheet should include debtors and accruals. In this example we would bring in the fees actually billed of £550,000. Let us assume there were expenses – stationery, telephone, library, etc. not paid at the year-end of £50,000. Tables 4.3 and 4.4 show the accounts on an '*accruals* basis' and indicate a much healthier profit of £50,000.

Table 4.3 Profit and loss account

£'000	Cash basis	Accruals basis
Income	400	550
Expenses	450	500
Profit/loss	–50	50

Table 4.4 Balance sheet

£'000	Cash basis	Accruals basis
Bank	–20	–20
Debtors		150
Creditors		–50
	–20	80
Capital		
Capital introduced	30	30
Profit/loss	–50	50
	–20	**80**

Arguably this second set of accounts, prepared on an accruals basis, shows a 'fairer' presentation of the firm's financial position. Overall the firm has assets of £80,000.

In 1998 the UK government announced that all professional firms had to properly account for work in progress (WIP) in their accounts. WIP was valued at cost and would exclude the WIP of the equity partners. If we assume that in addition to the two equity partners there were four solicitors, the amount of WIP to be included in the accounts was £65,000 as illustrated in Table 4.5.

Table 4.5 Value of WIP per printouts (at selling price)

	£
Partner 1	62,845
Partner 2	48,785
Partner total	**111,630**
Solicitor 1	29,742
Solicitor 2	32,526
Solicitor 3	25,845
Solicitor 4	18,325
Overall total	**218,068**
Less partners	–111,630
WIP of employed fee earners	106,438
Restate at cost (say) = Closing WIP	**65,000**

The income figure now comprises fees actually billed of £550,000 plus movement in work in progress of £65,000, giving total income £615,000. The firm is showing a profit of £115,000 on a *WIP basis* as illustrated in Table 4.6.

Table 4.6 Profit and loss account

£'000	**Cash basis**	**Accruals basis**	**Accruals basis with WIP**
Income	400	550	615
Expenses	450	500	500
Profit/loss	–50	50	115

Table 4.7 Balance sheet

£'000	**Cash basis**	**Accruals basis**	**Accruals basis with WIP**
Bank	–20	–20	–20
Debtors		150	150
WIP			65
Creditors		–50	–50
	–20	**80**	**145**
Capital			
Capital introduced	30	30	30
Profit/loss	–50	50	115
	–20	**80**	**145**

Once again, a good case can be put forward for saying that this set of accounts shows a much fairer picture of the firm's financial health. The partners have made a more respectable profit of £115,000 and the overall value of the assets of the firm is £145,000. If you were joining as a partner or planning on selling a share of the firm, the accounts show a more complete picture as more of the firm's assets have been included.

The final change took place in 2004, when, as part of the measures to improve financial reporting after the dot.com boom, changes were made to revenue recognition that resulted in UITF 40. A highly complex area, and one that accountants still do not fully agree on, UITF 40 requires revenue to be recognised where the firm had established a 'right to consideration' by the year-end. This was to be valued at selling price and crucially it included the time of equity partners. The new asset would be included as a debtor. Where work had been done, but no right to consideration had been created, the unbilled time would continue to be valued at cost and shown as WIP.

There has been extensive debate about work where the outcome was contingent, such as personal injury. However, if we take the simple WIP calculation in Table 4.5, and assume all of this unbilled time would need to be fully recognised under UITF 40 the effect would be to bring in accrued income of £218,000 as shown in Tables 4.8 and 4.9. The firm's income is now £550,000 + £218,000 = £768,000.

Table 4.8 Profit and loss account

£'000	Cash basis	Accruals basis	Accruals basis with WIP	Accruals with WIP on a UITF 40 basis
Income	400	550	615	768
Expenses	450	500	500	500
Profit/loss	–50	50	115	268

Table 4.9 Balance sheet

£'000	Cash basis	Accruals basis	Accruals basis with WIP	Accruals with WIP on a UITF 40 basis
Bank	–20	–20	–20	–20
Debtors		150	150	150
Accrued income				218
WIP			65	0
Creditors		–50	–50	–50
	–20	80	145	298
Capital				
Capital introduced	30	30	30	30
Profit/loss	–50	50	115	268
	–20	80	145	298

Why worry about all this?

This relatively simple example illustrates the huge impact on profits that the basis of accounting makes. The problem is that partners can all too easily assume that the profits shown in the accounts are available for them to draw, whereas the actual cash profit of their firm can be very different.

All firms in the UK now prepare their accounts on the basis of UITF 40, whereas firms in the US still work on a cash basis. If this firm was based in Manchester it would have recorded a profit of £268,000 and the partners may well have considered they were entitled to some drawings – after all they had made a profit of over £130,000 each. They might have felt quite comfortable financially, as there were assets approaching £300,000. They might have lost sight of the fact that in cash terms they had lost £50,000 and were overdrawn by £20,000. If the firm had been based in Michigan the partners would have been very aware of the cash position and would not be contemplating any drawings.

The point is illustrated by this recollection of an exchange in early negotiations between two leading UK and US firms:

> So. As part of the early merger negotiations, there was a videoconference between London and the States. In London, our team including our accountants, one of the big four firms. In the States their chairman and his team.
>
> Our accountants were explaining our accounts line by line. Their chairman looked increasingly baffled until the accountant came to the line 'cash at bank'. It was obviously very low. Maybe even overdrawn.
>
> 'So that's your profit?' says the Chairman. No, said thc accountant. Profit is £X. And then they took him back up to the revenue line to start again. Suddenly the Chair couldn't hold back any longer: 'hold on, hold on' he says. 'that's not profit, that's just bills!'
>
> He refused to accept that this was a legitimate basis for the calculation of profit.
>
> And so we adopted cash accounting. And the catharsis was amazing. Partners chased their own bills. Interim billing became the norm. In year one, there was a 7-figure merger dividend (as we called it). I can't remember the exact number but it was big.

The move towards LLP status and the move away from cash accounting to a WIP/UITF basis has therefore had a number of perhaps unintended results:

- Many partners, particularly in smaller firms, now find it more difficult to understand the balance sheet in their annual accounts – they have almost given up on the balance sheet.
- Unfortunately they also do not take much interest in the balance sheet in their firm's management accounts – which will be produced on a simple accruals basis. Many smaller firms do not even produce regular balance sheets, focusing instead on the profit and loss account.
- When gauging the level of profits available for drawings many firms overlook the proportion of their profits that are the result of WIP movements and fail to appreciate that their cash profits are not the same as their accounting profits. The partners can easily finish up overdrawing and increasing pressure on the bank as a result.
- Partners in UK law firms can have an approach to cash collection that is very different from the approach of their US equivalents. Firms that focus more on the real cash position, in particular those that relate partner drawings to cash collections, can achieve a very different bank position.

If we return to our partners based in Michigan and Manchester, the real answer is that neither of these balance sheets shows the correct position in terms of deciding what profits should be paid out to partners in the coming year. Cash flow forecasts are vital to assist with this. Management accounts and forecasts are invaluable tools for the management of your firm.

Management accounts

In the current economic climate the more partners fully understand the cash position of their firms the better. Whilst your firm's annual accounts must be prepared on a WIP/UITF 40 basis, it is for you to design the format of your firm's management accounts. Your aim should be the creation of a set of reports that best motivates your partners to focus on working capital – as well as profitability and income growth.

These will generally be prepared on an accruals basis – although income will be based on actual fees billed – but there may well be merit in also tracking cash collected in respect of each fee earner and even relating partner drawings to cash collections. Management accounts need to record what has happened up to the end of the last accounting period (they are normally prepared monthly or quarterly); however, they also need to include forecasts to assist with decisions to be taken which will affect the finances and profitability of the business in the next quarter and the year ahead.

One of the weaknesses the recession has exposed is the relatively weak financial information and controls many smaller firms still have. Most now produce a regular profit and loss account, but this will only provide headline figures and will not be fully understood by all the partners. It is unlikely to include a meaningful assessment of team or departmental profitability. Balance sheets will be produced rarely and cash flow projections will be even scarcer. Surprisingly, relatively few firms employ a qualified accountant. In a recent survey commissioned by the Legal Services Commission,[2] only 21 per cent of the 500 respondents employed an accountant. Even amongst firms with turnover over £1m, only 30 per cent employed an accountant.

2 *Legal Services Commission: Financial and Management Training Needs in Solicitor Firms* (March 2009). The sample was drawn from a cross section of firms that undertook both publicly funded and private work.

Case study

High Street multi-service firm with large non-geographic PI unit

How many partners does your firm have?	12
How many fee earners (including partners, paralegals and trainees) does your firm have?	92
What is your position in the firm?	Director of finance
Who is responsible for financial management?	Management board, which includes me, 4 equity partners, (including managing partner) and the other non-lawyer manager, the director of business development
Could you indicate what action your firm has had to take so far in dealing with the recession?	Lost about 70 people (245 down to 173 currently) in the last 18 months. Implemented a salary cut for remaining staff based upon: • 3% for staff earning up to £18k; • 5% for staff earning between £18k and £30k; and • 10% of salary above £30k. Salary will be restored by a payback scheme based upon the firm's cash collection target. 50% of the amount received in excess of that target will go into a pool and apportioned pro rata to those who have taken a salary reduction. Significant overhaul of costs in all areas, including premises costs by closing small offices; obtaining further competitive quotes in areas like accountancy and audit, stationery, window cleaning, office cleaning and sundries! Reducing cleaning frequencies. Focusing fee earners' minds on the importance of maximising recovery rates and cash collection. Constant re-forecasting of both profit & cash flow.
Do you have any particular suggestions as to things that have worked in helping your firm adjust?	The managing partner and HR partner (also an equity partner) have visited all the offices and explained the position to the staff and allowed them the chance to discuss the issues with them – before announcing the salary cut consultation. Equity members have met more frequently, to ensure they are kept up to date with the financial position. Dealing with the recession is largely about commitment and communication. We are lucky in having a balanced portfolio of income streams and about 84% of our budgeted income is non-cyclical, (e.g. personal injury) or counter-cyclical (e.g. business recovery & insolvency and dispute resolution): but we cannot escape the point that the recession reduced our income significantly until we adjusted our premises and salary costs.
Were there any ideas that have not worked?	Not yet. All things have worked to some extent so far.

Do you have any suggestions for managing debtors and WIP?	We have instituted a 'debt day' when the firm down-tools and fee earners phone all their debtors asking for payment. Financc provide them with a list by email, with space for comments as to what was agreed with the debtor, which is then returned to credit control for follow-up. Targets for this year are to be based on cash received rather than fees, which we hope will focus the fee earners' attention but it is early days yet on this. WIP is harder to deal with, except that we report recovery percentages and the factors that go into creating WIP, e.g. hours; but many business unit, (department) heads still do not buy in to the importance of monitoring what their staff are doing, so don't deal with the issues arising soon enough.
Do you have any suggestions for engaging partners and fee earners and getting them take action to reduce the amounts tied up in working capital?	The focus on cash collection (which we shadowed last year as a dummy run) has to be the key issue. Also, constantly bringing it up at partners' meetings emphasises its importance.
What are the main problem areas you face in making progress?	Lack of financial understanding on the part of too many fee earners, including partners. Communicating important & urgent issues across a multi-sited firm.
What are the main figures you now look at each month to monitor the financial health of the business?	Profit YTD and the month, fees, hours, cash received, cash balance, recovery rates
For how long do you expect the current recession to last, specifically in terms of the legal sector rather than the economy at large?	In my view, this is dependent upon the type of work that each firm undertakes. If it is in corporate & property, don't hold your breath. However, if you are in banking, insolvency, dispute resolution, have overseas work, or following the 2009 Budget, are in private client work, particularly taxation, you will find that work will turn up more quickly. So, I expect those firms to be seeing things coming round in Spring 2010: but for the rest of the economy, I would be looking at late 2010/early 2011.
Who in your firm is responsible for managing:	
(a) utilisation and fee earner payroll costs;	(a) Business unit heads
(b) leverage and secretarial to fee earner and support staff to fee earner ratios;	(b) Management board & business unit heads
(c) support staff payroll costs;	(c) Management board
(d) non-payroll overheads.	(d) Management board
Any other tips?	Focus on the big numbers, i.e. fees (hours & recoveries), salaries & premises costs: avoid distractions. Re-forecast constantly. Concentrate on cash rather than fees or even profit. Have a regular dialogue with your bank. Phone calls & emails are fine. Don't leave them in the dark – even if things are going OK. They may not know that things are OK and they certainly will not want a surprise if they are not. Ensure you keep perspective. Take time out for yourself occasionally. Play golf, or whatever else takes you away completely for a few hours every now and again!

Chapter 5

The main KPIs to monitor during a recession

The value of KPIs

Key performance indicators (KPIs) are now universally recognised as an essential means of monitoring the main financial drivers of a law firm. Most larger firms use them widely and smaller firms are increasingly trying to identify the main ones they must monitor.

It is really important for each firm to prioritise its KPIs and establish which ones are the most critical to its business. Every firm is different, and within firms, different offices or business units may have different financial drivers, so you need to decide which KPIs are most relevant to your firm at the present time. Furthermore, different KPIs are relevant as a firm moves through the economic cycle, so these should ideally be reviewed and updated – perhaps every year or so.

KPIs are useful as a management tool since what gets measured tends to get targeted. You need to minimise the opportunity for them to be misinterpreted or misunderstood by partners and fee earners – if you have an intranet or office manual it should include a clear definition and explanation of the main KPIs together with a timetable for their publication. Some pieces of financial information are best communicated daily; others weekly or monthly. Lawyers often prefer consistent communication on a regular basis regarding management information, rather than ad hoc reporting as and when the finance department feels this is appropriate. 'Less is more' – you should concentrate on no more than five KPIs at any one time. Information overload can easily happen, sometimes with disastrous effect if the partners become disengaged from managing their firm's finances.

To establish the relevant KPIs you need to decide what really matters for your firm. For many, *survival* is what matters most during a severe economic recession. Survival may have different interpretations, including:

- survival as an independent firm;
- not being taken over by another firm or forced to break up;
- not being subjected to restrictive banking covenants;
- being able to continue on a long-term path of strategic growth without being diverted by short-term working capital constraints;
- being able to continue to attract and retain the best lawyers; and
- being able to continue to win profitable business.

What matters therefore is good working capital management twinned with good profitability.

Working capital management

Working capital management encompasses the entire working capital cycle, from client care documentation, to matter acceptance procedures, billing practices, work in progress management to credit control.

Real working capital management needs to be effected through cultural or behavioural change rather than a set of policies and procedures. Partners need to appreciate that ultimately their clients will respect them as much for being attentive to administration, billing and credit control as for the technical legal aspects of their client relationships.

It is important to have an all-inclusive approach, reflecting the different drivers of different parts of the business.

The fruits of working capital management are strong cash collections, therefore it is important to report and to focus on these. Within the field of working capital, there are many KPIs we could use, but three are critical:

- cash collections;
- debtor days; and
- work in progress days.

Cash collections

These are the most obvious measure of successful working capital, so we should start by defining them. Whilst it is important to monitor total collections, including VAT and disbursements, since the VAT will be forwarded to HMRC and all disbursements must be paid out straightaway to counsel, agents, etc., what is really relevant to a firm's cash flow is the *fees* collected each day.

The accounts or credit control department needs to be very clearly focused on collecting all amounts due from clients, so for them, it is total collections which are relevant. Ideally total collections should be monitored on a daily basis, and there should be two sets of targets. The first should be a stretching target, based on getting back to debtor days of, say, 60 days at the end of the month in question. The second would then be a more realistic target, used to set cash flow forecasts, based on the recent experience of the firm in terms of the percentage of bills settled in the month of billing, the following month, the next month, and so on.

Your accounts department or credit controller will then be motivated by calculations showing the average collections received per day for the month to date, the daily average required to achieve these target figures by the end of the current month, etc.

It is important to publicise successes achieved by the accounts or credit control team as their work is crucial to the smooth running of the firm.

Debtor days

Put simply, debtor days are the number of days' worth of fee income that it takes the firm to collect its debts from clients.

Debtor days can be measured by reference to fees billed; or to fees, disbursements and VAT billed; or to fees and disbursements only billed. Sometimes different methodologies will be more appropriate for different businesses, but it is important that the same criteria are applied to the numerator and denominator of the calculation for consistency.

Normally debtor days are worked out using 365 days. Some firms use the number of working days available; however, banks calculate interest on bank holidays and weekends so it is technically more correct to use the total number of days in the year. It is generally preferable for debtor days to be calculated using the countback method, taking the most recent month's fee income first, rather than averaging fee income over the past year. This is particularly relevant for law firms where there are sizeable billing peaks during each quarter or at the end of the financial year, or for firms where a large proportion of their fee income is billed at significant points relating to client transactions. Until recent years, many partners left far too much of their billing until the last month, or sometimes the last few days of the financial year – and some partners are still guilty of this today. This has a distorting impact on debtor days unless they were calculated using the countback method. The introduction of e-billing, and a gradual migration of billing practices towards interim or monthly billing has helped enormously, but there are still many firms with an uneven billing profile by month so for these, the use of the countback method is necessary.

Table 5.1 illustrates the following example. At the end of January total debtors were £258,750.

Table 5.1 Debtor days

Debtor days	**£**	**Days**
Debtors at end January (excluding VAT and disbursements)	225,000	
Fees (excluding VAT and disbursements)		
January	62,500	31
December	85,600	31
November (balance)	76,900	25
(November fees were £92,000 so the balance represents 25 days or 76,900/92,000 x 30 days)	0	87

The table takes the total debtors at the end of the month, excludes VAT and then deducts each month's fees until zero is reached.

Debtor days can be measured in absolute terms; however what is important for working capital improvement is continuous incremental reductions in debtor days. It can be useful to use an incremental approach with partners being informed of the impact on the firm's cash flows of a reduction in debtor days of, for example, three days.

Debtor days should be published at a business unit level, or an office level, to all partners and fee earners in the firm, each month. Comparisons with figures from the previous months can be beneficial along with benchmarking. Some firms circulate charts showing the last six months' figures, on both a firm-wide and a team basis.

You may well need to recognise the differences between different offices and clients. Some clients may be awarded a discount for prompt payment, others may have most of their fees paid immediately upon completion of a matter.

Figure 5.1 illustrates a wide variation in debtor days using answers drawn from the LMS Benchmarking Survey 2008 – a median of 48 is low and must be treated with a degree of care as the sample size is relatively small.

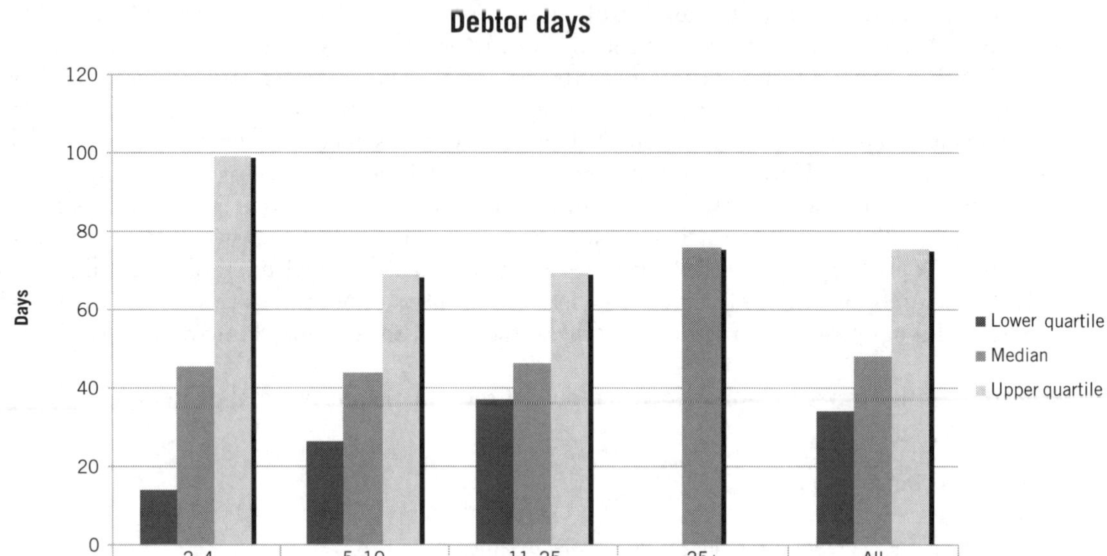

	2–4	5–10	11–25	25+	All
Lower quartile	14	26	37		34
Median	45	44	46	76	48
Upper quartile	99	69	69		75

Figure 5.1 Debtor days

Work in progress days

Work in progress days show the length of time taken for work to be billed. It is a vital step in the working capital cycle.

Some firms have low levels of work in August and December, owing to holidays, therefore the points made above regarding the countback method are relevant here too, in order not to arrive at a distorted figure. Similarly, work in progress days should be calculated by reference to 365 days rather than being based on working days. For consistency, work in progress days should compare the value of work recorded at agreed rates with the value of unbilled time at agreed rates.

Work in progress days reports should be published monthly to all partners, and often fee earners as well. The most relevant figure is not the absolute number of days, but the trend compared to previous periods.

Comparisons between business units or offices will be relevant up to a point. It is important to recognise that different parts of the firm may have different billing patterns. Major personal injury and medical negligence cases, for example, might not be billed for several years, whereas company and commercial work should be billed each month.

Again the publication of successes is important and firms should consider circulating 'sinners lists' ('sinners' being the partners or fee earners with the largest work in progress balances over three months old, each month, in descending order). Even missing timesheets play a part in work in progress days. The later time is captured on matter files, the greater the likelihood it will be missed at the billing cut off, and the longer it will then take to be billed to the client the following month.

Figure 5.2 summarises WIP days from the LMS Benchmarking Survey 2008.

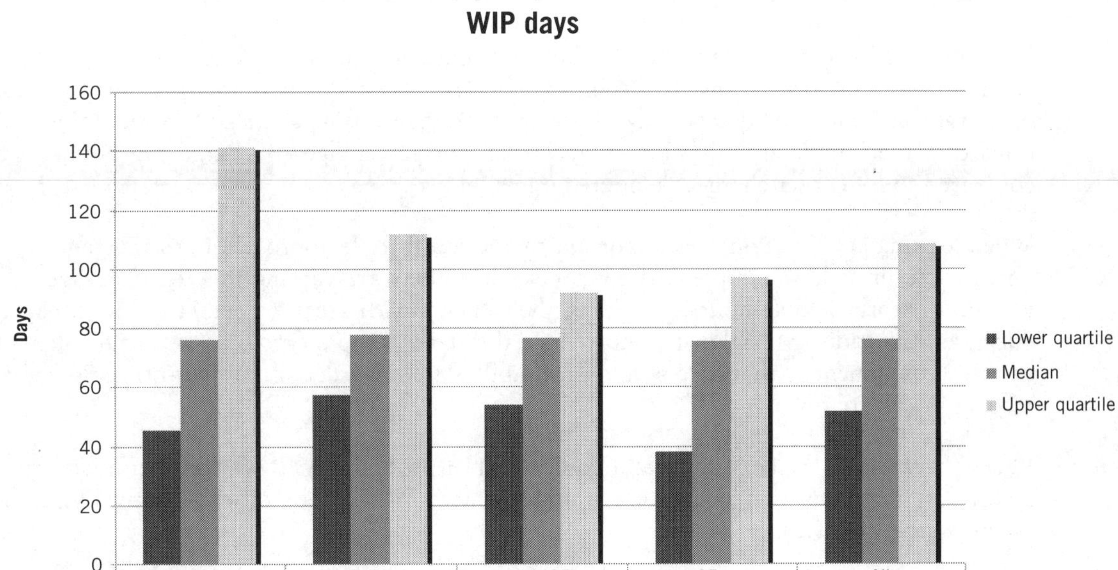

	2–4	5–10	11–25	25+	All
Lower quartile	45	57	54	38	52
Median	76	78	76	76	76
Upper quartile	141	112	92	97	109

Figure 5.2 WIP days

Interpretation of working capital KPIs

Interpretation of these three KPIs is key: lawyers often prefer an explanatory paragraph and coloured charts to a table of figures with no commentary or explanation. Every firm is different and it is the responsibility of each finance director or accountant to gauge the best way of communicating effectively with their partners.

Behavioural aspects are pivotal. Working capital management should be an active component of the appraisal process for partners and for senior lawyers. Larger firms might consider a link with performance so that partners with better working capital management generally are more highly remunerated than those with weaker working capital performance.

The role of the finance professional in a practice is to set out best practice in working capital, and then motivate their partners and fee earners to achieve – then maintain – this standard. It will certainly pay dividends in cash flow terms.

The subject of collections targets has been debated at length within many firms. In some firms, the operation of group cash collections targets can work well. Some professional services firms also link the payment of drawings payments to these, although others find such an approach divisive.

Profitability – the next two KPIs

Profitability KPIs can be established for both revenues and costs, and one of the most important is utilisation. Some firms translate this into *x* hours per day and believe that providing the number of chargeable hours recorded per day is at *x* or more, their business will still be profitable and well utilised. Others look at utilisation in terms of the percentage of chargeable hours recorded compared to fee earner chargeable hours targets.

When looking at utilisation, it is important to adopt a flexible approach. In the current economic crisis, some firms have adopted a four-day week. Others are varying this to encourage their fee earners to work flexible hours, providing their clients with greater flexibility. The other key to effective utilisation is to take steps to reduce the fixed component of costs and to increase the variable component so that success and profitability are rewarded, but under-utilisation and poor recovery rates are not.

Recovery rates are the next important component of profitability. If we consider a law firm with a cost base that is fairly fixed, the profit and loss account will look different according to the fee income (see Table 5.2).

Table 5.2 Net profit in relation to fee income

All figures in £millions	Scenario 1	Scenario 2	Scenario 3
Fee income	80	81	85
Costs	56	56	56
Net profit	24	25	29
Profit margin %	30%	31%	34%
Increase from first scenario		4%	21%

Let us assume that the recovery rate is 80 per cent (scenario 1) so that the value of chargeable time recorded (excluding movements in work in progress) is £100m. If costs remain constant and the recovery rate improves by just 1 per cent to 81 per cent (scenario 2), the additional income is all translated into incremental profits for the partners. The additional fee income of £1m results in increased profits of £1m or 4 per cent. In scenario 3, when the recovery rate improved to 85 per cent, this has a massive impact on profits and improves the net profits for partners by 21 per cent to £29m. Similarly reductions in recovery rates have a marked downward impact on profits, at the margin.

So how do we effect improvements in recovery rates? The first step is to understand profitability at a client or matter level. To do this we need to ensure that all time is captured promptly, completely and that the narratives are sufficiently detailed to allow the partner – and eventually the client – to see the value of the work done.

Too often timesheets are entered late, after the final bill has been sent to the client. This 'lost' fee income represents lost profits for the partners of the firm. It is a good idea to check with all of the fee earners working on a particular matter that all their time has been entered up to date before finalising the last bill for that matter.

Circulation of missing timesheets lists each week is also a good idea. Many fee earners use electronic timers to record their time these days, but there are still a handful of fee earners, even in larger firms, whom we might describe as 'dinosaurs', who dictate timesheets to their secretaries at the end of each week or fortnight. All it takes is for the secretary to be on holiday for a fortnight and a substantial amount of time is either lost or billed to the client several weeks later than necessary.

Many property transactions involve post-completion time. When preparing bills for all real estate matters, ensure the person preparing the bill checks to see how much work should be anticipated for post-completion work including tax compliance, compilation of bibles, etc.

We have also seen a tendency for some fee earners, particularly those fairly new to the law, to under-record their time because they genuinely believe that a particular piece of work should not have taken them so long, and they do not wish to appear as being 'slow' to their reporting partner. This is another behavioural point, but an important one because of its direct impact on the recovery rate and on profits. It is important that all fee earners are encouraged to record their time as accurately as possible, and not to feel pressured to under-record their time. It is then for the partner finalising the bill to the client to decide the appropriate amount to be billed on to the client for each piece of work.

The following dilemmas also have an impact on recovery rates, and profitability:

- How do I ensure that I organise my working day most efficiently so as to minimise telephone and email interruptions?
- Who pays for the real cost of an interrupted phone call from another client?
- Can I charge my client for travelling time? Many clients will accept a 50 per cent charge for travelling rather than a nil charge.
- Can I charge for work done on the way to/from the office on the train?

Another aspect to consider, if you cannot recover travelling time and this is significant, is whether it is more efficient for all concerned, as well as being 'greener', to have a telephone or video conference call in lieu of a face to face meeting.

Some fee earners are reluctant to charge for research in the belief that it might not be chargeable to the client. However, it is often better for this time to be recorded and then for the matter partner to make an informed judgement as to its recoverability rather than for the fee earners not to record the time. Consistency and completeness of time recording are absolutely vital for any law firm. Ideally firms should have a time recording policy that is issued (and then re-circulated periodically) to all staff. This will provide a framework for time recording and will make it easier for bills to be rendered that are complete and consistent, particularly when fee earners from different practice areas or different offices are working on a particular project together.

In addition to utilisation and recovery rates, the last main contributor to profitability, as already outlined, is the cost base of the firm – payroll and overheads. In most smaller firms, exercising control over costs is delegated to the managing partner with support from the accountant although other partners would often have a view.

Case study

Medium-sized, multi-niche practice

How many partners does your firm have?	18
How many fee earners (including partners, paralegals and trainees) does your firm have?	46
What is your position in the firm?	Chief executive
Who is responsible for financial management?	Chief executive, in consultation with management committee (comprising three equity partners and head of Finance) and the various heads of department.
Could you indicate what action your firm has had to take so far in dealing with the recession?	1. Implementation of a redundancy programme – Summer/Autumn 2008 which led to the redundancy of 15 posts, principally in conveyancing and general support services disciplines. 2. Greater analysis of expenditure plans. 3. Greater focus on all other non-property related Departments working harder to at least deliver their stated fee and profitability targets. 4. Greater focus on delegation of tasks to the most appropriate level of fee earner.
Do you have any particular suggestions as to things that have worked in helping your firm adjust?	1. Face up and be realistic and don't delay taking action in the vain hope that 'somehow things will just improve!' 2. Take the opportunity to review whether it is possible to improve service, speed up delivery of client services and perform tasks in a more efficient and cost effective way. 3. Be open and transparent and communicate with the staff – they know it is tough out there so will understand the rationale of the need to take even the toughest of decisions especially if we communicate with them openly, effectively and frequently. Our experience is that staff have greater empathy with the situation we are facing than we sometimes give them credit for.
Were there any ideas that have not worked?	We have not implemented lots of ideas, just a small number and focused all of our energies on these, the outcome being we have not had any failed ideas – so far!

<table>
<tr><td>Do you have any suggestions for managing debtors and WIP?</td><td>1. Managing debt and WIP effectively does not require the mind of an Einstein or the wizardry of a Merlin! There are in my view two crucial and fundamental points all fee earners, including the most seasoned partners always need to bear in mind:

(a) Effective debt management starts not when a bill has remained unpaid for 30 or more days but at the time the client is first engaged – get the understanding between fee earner and client right at this stage and debt risk should be minimised.

(b) Responsibility for ensuring the bill is paid lies squarely with the fee earner and is not a responsibility that can or should be shunted on to Accounts, Credit Control or elsewhere.

2. Ensure that terms of business support and complement rather than contradict what is said on bills, statements and client care letters – it is very common for example for a bill to say 'payable within 30 days' and the Terms and Conditions to say something contrary!

3. Managing debt is about taking responsibility and in particular about the equity partners setting the example. It serves no purpose whatever for partners to pontificate about the need to free up lock up when in some cases they are the worst debt and WIP management offenders!

4. Reserve the right in the Terms to charge the client an extra £25 plus VAT for each and every payment reminder sent and certainly reserve the right to charge interest on late payments, even if only rarely used.

Remember that clients are not usually affronted by being chased for unpaid bills providing the 'chase' is made politely and tactfully. In terms of WIP management there is little new to say – it is all a question of fee earners and their immediate fee supervisors exercising common financial sense and this means ensuring that all fee earners are educated in the 'business of law' – and by that I mean the simple inter-relationships of billing, debt, WIP and payment (cash flow). The tried and tested methods of regular interim billing, getting bills out on time, preferably prefaced by a call to the client to say 'the bill is on the way, etc., etc.; ensuring that clients and not the partners fund unbilled disbursements; ensuring there are sufficient monies held on client account; only setting up standing orders, etc. where the bill is paid in full over a maximum period of six months; ensuring that in most wills and probate and most residential and commercial property jobs the firm's fees are deducted from balances held on behalf of the client.</td></tr>
<tr><td>Do you have any suggestions for engaging partners and fee earners and getting them take action to reduce the amounts tied up in working capital?</td><td>Education, education, education.

The most potent reminder is simply to point out to partners that making a concerted, continuous effort to free up just a proportion of cash locked up in the business in the form of debt and WIP would produce results sufficient to wipe out the need for any overdraft or other form of borrowing!</td></tr>
</table>

What are the main problem areas you face in making progress?	Lack of commercial acumen and understanding of just how fast the legal services market is changing. The profession simply must learn to accept that it is a business that simply happens to deliver legal services as opposed to 'widgets' and that increasingly lawyers need to be businessmen and women first and lawyers second!
What are the main figures you now look at each month to monitor the financial health of the business?	Profit contributions made by each of the departments, cash flow, billing, movement in WIP, debtors, unbilled disbursement balances and new matter starts primarily. We pay limited attention to expenditure given most significant expenditure heads are to a great extent fixed.
For how long do you expect the current recession to last, specifically in terms of the legal sector rather than the economy at large?	We are planning on the recession lasting at least another full annual business planning cycle and for us that is 1 April 09 to 31 March 2010.
Who in your firm is responsible for managing:	
(a) utilisation and fee earner payroll costs;	(a) CEO and management committee
(b) leverage and secretarial to fee earner and support staff to fee earner ratios;	(b) Ditto
(c) support staff payroll costs;	(c) Ditto
(d) non-payroll overheads.	(d) Ditto
Any other tips?	There is no point in using WIP, debtor management or any other financial management controls and disciplines as occasional tools with which to beat fee earners. The key in my view is ensuring that fee earners fully understand their personal 'business of law' responsibilities and this starts with effective induction for new staff and ensuring there is a continuous process of education for fee earners at all levels.

Chapter 6

The starting point for credit control – getting the initial agreement with the client right[1]

The key to good working capital management lies at the start of every matter. Communicating the value of your efforts to clients and managing their expectations in respect of costs and billing should enable you to maximise billing potential and reduce aged debt and disbursement levels.

The engagement letter – the key first stage

All clients, private and commercial, approach legal services with concern about the potential cost. Discussing costs openly and transparently should be seen as an opportunity to come to an agreement that is satisfactory to both parties. Your aim should be to keep your WIP, bills and paid-bills cycle to a minimum by always ensuring that a client is aware of their costs liability at all stages of a matter, and never giving a client cause to delay paying a bill. This aspect of your service is so important for firm and client that every firm should have a billing protocol by which all its members must abide, without exception.

Agreeing how costs are to be assessed and the method and timing of billing with the client at the outset, and encapsulating these terms in a carefully worded terms of engagement letter, the client care letter, should govern all subsequent financial arrangements in respect of that matter.

The client care letter itself should be a contemporaneous record of the discussions with your client, setting out clearly and concisely what you have agreed to do, what you will not be covering, the method and terms of billing for that work, plus the other requirements of rule 2.03. Most firms send separate terms and conditions with the client care letter, referring to any conditions specifically affecting the retainer in the letter, including any conditions relating to costs. Many larger firms have a fairly concise umbrella client care letter, with terms and conditions set out as an Appendix, which is then followed up by a simple email confirming specifics relating to each matter as and when required.

In most situations the existence of a signed client care letter and terms of engagement provides the framework to enable a fee earner or an accounts department to request monies on account, submit bills and collect payment promptly.

Issues must not be fudged in costs discussions, but be dealt with clearly and in unambiguous terms, including those such as whether part of the first interview is free, when legal services funding comes into operation and its full implications, whether the charges quoted are inclusive or exclusive of VAT, whether you charge for internal meetings on a matter and the way in which items such as letters in and phone calls will be dealt with. Tell your client about any anticipated disbursements and when you are going to require payment of them. Too often, muddles and

1 We would like to thank Heather Stewart for her assistance in preparing this chapter.

misunderstandings about payment terms, amounts to be billed for photocopying and other disbursements, and all other manner of details within the billing process, arise through a lack of clarity and understanding at the outset. Make sure that information on costs is given in language and terms that are not overly technical but are clearly understood by all clients.

Agree how you are going to bill and discuss appropriate alternative methods of billing. If you are offering a fixed price or giving an estimate up to a certain stage, be precise as to the terms of reference of the work that is included in that price, and equally what is to be excluded, and set them out clearly in your letter. Are you covering tax advice for instance? Even with fixed fees, you must explain to your client both in your discussions and in your client care letter that further fees may have to be considered where the scope of the work varies materially from that originally described to arrive at the fixed fee.

For both private and commercial clients, the nature of the work (its scale or complexity or both) can vary considerably after the initial outline of the work is provided to the lawyer. Where work done varies markedly, and will result in an escalation of work required and therefore costs, it is important to explain this clearly to the client and to confirm it in your client care letter.

If you cannot give a firm estimate, give one within a range of figures. Be aware of clients' interpretation of the word 'estimate'; few distinguish it from a quotation.

Ensure that all estimates are realistic. In the consumer-focused decision in *Tracey Reynolds* v. *Stone Rowe Brewer (a Firm)* [2008] EWHC 497 (QB), it was held that Stone Rowe Brewer, despite giving regular costs updates and having done the work charged for, should be drawn back to their original estimate plus 15 per cent.

Make sure that your fee earners do not significantly under-quote to secure work and then increase their estimate as the case progresses, where nothing material has changed in the retainer since the original estimate was given.

Agree when you are going to bill, and stick to your agreement. Interim billing, where appropriate, should be agreed whenever possible. If you submit a bill shortly after doing the work, the client will remember what you have done and their perception of its value will be greater. For firms, interim billing is a great help for cash flow and obviates the need to purge bill. Because it is little and often, fee earners are less likely to feel the need to write off time to keep the client happy. Agree to bill on a time basis rather than when the matter has reached a significant stage – the latter will mean that a significant amount of costs will also have accrued. Agree weekly, monthly, quarterly, etc. and then stick to your agreement, even if only a small amount of time has been recorded.

Make sure that the person conducting the initial interview is aware of the impact that different types of billing will have on your cash flow and the profitability of the work. Remember too that even if you handle costs issues well, there will be others in your firm who do not. Billing protocols and specific procedures that must be followed are the only way of ensuring firm-wide consistency. You have to be prepared to train and to use sanctions if fee earners and partners, breach your codes of practice.

Monies on account and credit checks

It is always sensible in these recessionary times to ask clients for money on account of costs and to pay disbursements in advance. No matter how well you know a client, they can be made redundant or worse be declared bankrupt or a commercial client may go into administration or liquidation leaving you with an irrecoverable WIP or a bill. It is sensible to run a credit check on all prospective clients, private and commercial. The results can then dictate the wording included within the client care letter relating to monies on account of costs and the payment of bills.

Furthermore, do not rely on past payment history. Even if costs were paid successfully in the first matter, it is a good idea to run a further credit check to be sure that the client is still a good credit risk if the client returns with a new instruction after a period of a year or so.

Costs updates

Communication about costs should take place not only at the beginning of a matter but throughout. Rule 2.03 states that you must give your client the best information possible about the likely overall cost of a matter both at the outset and, when appropriate, as the matter progresses. Do not assume that a client will realise that costs are mounting, even if they are aware of the work you are doing for them. You must always inform them on a regular basis and frequently if costs are accumulating quickly, in litigation for example, where costs can escalate rapidly immediately before and during a trial. Remember to notify your client of any changes in hourly rates, when a trainee qualifies for example, or the different rates for anyone else involved in the work.

Where you can only bill on the conclusion of a lengthy matter, send clients regular statements of accrued costs. Discuss the regularity of these with the client at the outset. Now that most practice management systems have reporting tools which can generate emails or reports automatically, it is quite straightforward to produce a report showing the latest position for work in progress, unbilled disbursements, outstanding fees and monies on account of costs to large clients each week.

For some commercial clients, the client care letter will provide for weekly cost updates, matter budgets and regular reporting to the client on work in progress and disbursements. If these provisions are adhered to, there should be no nasty surprises for the client when the final bill is presented to them.

However, in the majority of matters, although fee earners give the requisite information on costs to a client at the outset, many fail to get back to their client before an estimate is exceeded or to review costs as originally agreed. The result is usually an unhappy client who has not necessarily anticipated that costs have mounted to the extent they have and you have problems collecting the amount you would like to charge. Make sure that you review the rule 2 requirements when supervising work – it is a requirement of rule 5 that you do. Use your IT to prompt you before an estimate runs out by setting it to flag at say 75 per cent or 80 per cent of the estimate. Get back to the client as soon as you know whether a matter is not going to follow the anticipated path that you set out in your client care letter. Renegotiate costs if you are able to. It is only fair to give the client the opportunity to decide whether to proceed.

Often, for private clients, transactions will be very personal to them and have an emotional significance in addition to the substance of the work being done. It is particularly important in these types of transactions that you are very clear with the client about the potential costs involved in particular courses of action, and that they understand the ramifications of their decisions during the course of a matter. The client care letter provides the framework for this to be set out clearly with no opportunity for misunderstandings. Carrying out cost-benefit analyses with clients when reviewing costs with them as a matter proceeds also helps them focus their minds as to whether it is worth their while proceeding.

All information about costs must be confirmed in writing to your client; an informal chat is not enough. Make sure that all your correspondence is unambiguous to avoid the risk of delayed payment. If you send a series of letters about costs, ensure that they are consistent and present a short summary of previous information. Always keep costs information readily apparent on a file so that any other fee earner taking over or working on the file is aware of the agreed costs position and does not run up costs outside that agreement.

For the rest of this chapter we will look at the essential ingredients of client care documentation from a working capital rather than a regulatory perspective. In summary the client care letter and your terms and conditions of business should set out all aspects of billing that impinge upon working capital.

Billing

If you have discussed costs with your client at stages throughout the matter and involved them in the way it has progressed, then when you send a bill that accords with the terms of your financial agreement, most clients will pay. The narrative should be sufficiently lengthy to communicate the value of work you have undertaken but not overly lengthy and not in prosaic language. Above all, the bill should include a breakdown of the way it has been calculated. Unless you have previously agreed this format, 'To professional charges for advising you on ... £5,000.00', is not enough. Omitting information about the calculation of the amount is a common failing and one that upsets or irritates clients. Give details of the hours worked and by whom and the appropriate rates, numbers of phone calls, etc. Include them in a schedule if you prefer. Some practitioners do not send these details initially but supply them on subsequent request from the client. However, that is merely delaying payment of the bill. If you have any doubts, discuss it with the client beforehand.

Getting the bill addressed to the correct person at the correct entity

It is vital to have correct details for your client on file, and if a commercial client, a record of the main client contact. Their current address and postcode is essential, along with email address and telephone number, including mobile phone numbers for private clients. For commercial clients, contact details for relevant secretaries or their accounts department are also important. It is always worth speaking to a client's accounts department to see whether your invoice can be brought forward to their next payment run.

Again for commercial clients, keep a record of the name and full contact details of the person responsible for approving invoices for payment. Too often time is lost when bills lie buried in the in-trays of the main client contact, before your credit controller discovers several weeks later that they have not been passed on to the person responsible for approving the bill. If that person is then on holiday or away on business for a few weeks, debtor days can balloon by a month or more.

Where a third party is responsible for paying your client's bill, for example a landlord client where the tenant is responsible or a bank client when a customer is paying, ensure there is a clear note on the file of the name of the payee and their address.

The address to which the bill should be sent is crucial. Too often I see bills being queried then reversed and reissued for commercial clients because the billing address was not specified clearly at the start of the matter, or because the bill is now to be raised to another group entity with a different VAT rate. This is important because omitting this vital piece of information can extend debtor days by a month unnecessarily.

Including relevant details on the face of the bill

The client care letter should also set out precisely the information which is required by the client on the face of the bill. Many commercial clients impose additional requirements which need to be satisfied before the bill can be approved for payment. These include supplementary financial information regarding the bill, the format of the bill, reference or purchase order numbers, the currency and exchange rate of the bill, the level of detail regarding disbursements, the level of detail regarding narrative, etc.

For example, some clients pay 50 per cent for travelling time. This should be set out clearly in the client care letter so that there is no room for doubt on the matter. Some require the time narratives to follow a particular format, others do not wish to be billed for internal meetings. Whatever the requirements, they should be automated within the firm's time recording and billing system as far as possible (often through the use of user defined fields) and should be stated clearly within the client care letter.

Timing of bills

The quid quo pro of making an agreement with your client must be that you get paid promptly and this has to be emphasised to your client at the outset as well. Never give a client an excuse for late payment – stick to your agreement. Send the bill when agreed because your client will be waiting for it and will view its non-arrival as a sign of your inefficiency and unreliability. Being too busy or there being insufficient time recorded to warrant raising a bill is not an excuse. Let the client know why it has not been sent. Always send bills as soon as practically possible on the conclusion of a matter, when your client can still remember the value of what you have done for them. Clients expect prompt delivery, they want to pay the bill and move on with their lives. Sending a bill three months later is also an indication of inefficiency and suggests that you are not concerned with being paid quickly. Billing protocols should include rules on the delivery of bills and the way billing is handled should also be discussed in supervision meetings.

The client care letter should specify how often bills are to be raised – periodic, upon completion, interim billing after pre-set milestones, or some combination thereof. The client is then bound by this. Ideally all clients should be migrated to monthly billing. However in practice I appreciate that this is not necessarily feasible for all clients or all types of transactions. The most frequent reason for not billing monthly is that the matter can only be billed upon completion. This tends to be true of contingent work, but does not apply to the majority of work either for corporate or for private clients.

Most law firms have spikes in cash flows owing to quarterly rent and VAT payments, six-monthly income tax payments, annual professional indemnity and law society practising certificates payments, etc. Therefore every effort to achieve a more even profile of billing through the year, and throughout each quarter, will have a marked positive impact upon cash flows.

We have observed that partners will readily agree to monthly billing as a principle; however, too often they breach this principle in practice. But this is no longer necessary. As with many aspects of law firm financial management, behavioural aspects are important. We believe that much as partners might wish to raise bills to clients more frequently, they have a 'fear' that to do so would not be acceptable to the client. However, if monthly billing is set out in the client care letter, the principle has already been established with the client. The client care letter should therefore include reference to monthly or interim billing, on a quarterly basis or on the occurrence of agreed milestones until the final bill is issued. Far from being offended by this, most clients will treat this as evidence of good financial practice. Partners should take as much pride in their working capital management with clients as with the quality of their legal work. In the long run, clients will respect them for this. Anecdotally, we have seen that accounting firms are far more up front and proactive with their clients regarding working capital issues.

Although monthly billing is important, inevitably, following the introduction of UITF 40, there is a specific need and opportunity to bill out all non-contingent work at the end of the financial year. So, six weeks in advance of the year-end, partners have the opportunity to contact their clients, to explain this billing out of work in progress to their clients, so that at the time the end of the year arrives, there is no element of surprise or shock when the client receives a bill bringing all matters completely up to date.

There is often pressure on fee earners to hit year-end billing targets and there is a consequent rush to bill at that time. However, care must be taken to ensure that such bills accord with client agreements. Purge billing as the year-end approaches, or to improve cash flow, should be avoided unless you take care not to upset clients. If you have entered into an agreement on costs with your client, and you have stuck to it by billing as you agreed, there should be no need either to have the 'purge' or to send a bill to your client at that time. The bill will not be anticipated and will be seen as outside the terms of the agreement.

Do not send any bill that might surprise a client – always discuss it with them first. This provides an opportunity to remind the client of the work that has been involved and to obtain their agreement as to the amount. We would prefer partners to telephone the client, at the point they are about to finalise the bill, to take them through the bill, its components, in order that there are no nasty surprises when the client receives the bill. Clients maintain that this is an important step psychologically – when the bill arrives, they will be expecting it and you are likely to be paid reasonably quickly. If you do not make the phone call, the bill may be a shock to your client who will put it to the bottom of the pile where it will remain until you have the embarrassment of chasing it.

Discounting bills rarely has a positive influence on clients: '£950.00 but say £900.00', for example. Clients merely wonder why you have not just charged them £900.00 in the first place. Instead, contact the client in advance and agree the amount with them, and then, as with all bills, send the bill promptly.

Payment terms

Most firms set out their payment terms in their terms and conditions which accompany their client care letter, including the payment of interest on late payment if you intend to charge it. The majority either have payment terms of 30 days or their fees are payable immediately upon presentation of the invoice. Setting appropriate payment terms is something to think about – perhaps different parts of the practice should have different payment terms. There are some large corporate clients who have standard terms of business which apply to all their suppliers; in any event the payment terms should be set out clearly in the initial client care documentation.

But the client care letter and terms and conditions should go further than this. As well as setting out the payment terms, they should also state that, if the client queries a part of the bill, they remain liable to settle the remainder of the bill in accordance with these terms. Too often we have seen clients query a small component of a bill, using this as an excuse not to settle the majority of it.

Disbursements

The amount of disbursements should be set out in the client care letter or notified to clients as soon as it appears that they will become payable. Wherever possible they should be collected in before the payment has to be made on behalf of the client. If that is not possible, a disbursement only bill should be sent immediately after payment has been made. At worst, they should always be included on an interim or the final bill. Many partners shy away from billing disbursements. Some fear that it might seem trivial and would upset clients. In fact the opposite is true because corporate clients will view this as businesslike behaviour. Clients would not act as a banker to their legal representatives. It is of course important to be totally transparent with regard to disbursements and to recharge those disbursements to clients at cost.

Bank account details

The client care documentation should include the bank account to which payment should be sent. Clients should be encouraged to send payments electronically where possible. Many law firms do not accept payment in cash owing to the anti-money laundering legislation. In some cases, for private clients, this needs to be explained to the client in advance of the bill being rendered.

Client queries

If a client does not pay within the time specified in your terms and conditions, the first questions to ask should be:

- Has the bill actually been sent?
- Is the client dissatisfied with the way the matter has been handled?

If the latter, appropriate steps to deal with the client's grievance should be taken immediately.

For commercial clients, queries on bills is another area in which a lack of clarity can cause debtor days to inflate unnecessarily. In the same way that I avoid my pile of ironing at home, some partners have been known to put off difficult correspondence with commercial clients, including responding to their bill queries. But this is important as it is another component of the working capital cycle which is often overlooked.

All firms need effective credit control which should begin with managing the billing agreement with clients at the outset. Responsibility for debt collection is often a grey area. In some firms, the cashier undertakes debt collection while in others it remains the responsibility of the fee earner. Neither is usually satisfactory because cashiers are too busy to prioritise it while a busy fee earner will be fearful of upsetting the client. It is usually cost effective for a firm to employ a credit controller whose sole function is to chase debts systematically and without interference.

Case study

London office of top 70 US law firm

How many partners does your firm have?	Globally around 230; 20 in the UK
How many fee earners (including partners, paralegals and trainees) does your firm have?	Globally around 500; 60 in the UK
What is your position in the firm?	Director of administration
Who is responsible for financial management?	Director of administration
Could you indicate what action your firm has had to take so far in dealing with the recession?	The firm in the US had a redundancy programme in the latter part of 2008 and spring of 2009. In the UK, which is growing, redundancy has, in effect, occurred by support staff recruitment freeze.
Do you have any particular suggestions as to things that have worked in helping your firm adjust?	We have focused, and continue to focus not only on ensuring that those who have been released are supported by us contacting local employers, but also ensuring that remaining staff realise their importance and value. Various staff initiatives in place, e.g. 'bring in your children day'.
Were there any ideas that have not worked?	Not that I can think of, but I am sure there are. We are being aggressive on cash management, but not that well.
Do you have any suggestions for managing debtors and WIP?	In the UK we have departmental finance partners who act as Billing Bulldogs. In the US drawings can be linked to client/matter management.
Do you have any suggestions for engaging partners and fee earners and getting them take action to reduce the amounts tied up in working capital?	I don't think there's much magic to this. We have an ongoing 'advanced profit distribution initiative' but you can only do this very occasionally. Other than that, keep talking to people all the time.
What are the main problem areas you face in making progress?	Mainly, as I imagine for other firms, getting through to the less commercial partners about their role in making cash come in.
What are the main figures you now look at each month to monitor the financial health of the business?	• Client service time (value added) • Billings • Collections • Cash expenditure
For how long do you expect the current recession to last, specifically in terms of the legal sector rather than the economy at large?	I can't see major improvements until 2010, although there seems now (April 2009) to be slightly less 'herd panic' in the air.
Who in your firm is responsible for managing:	
(a) utilisation and fee earner payroll costs;	(a) Departmental partner in charge
(b) leverage and secretarial to fee earner and support staff to fee earner ratios;	(b) Departmental manager and office director of administration
(c) support staff payroll costs;	(c) Office director of administration
(d) non-payroll overheads.	(d) Responsible support director

Chapter 7

Debtors and WIP management

Managing debtors and work in progress is vital to any business, and especially so to professional services firms. In the same way that a pilates teacher might urge you to strengthen your core muscles, the working capital is the 'core' of any business and it needs to be as lean and as strong as possible, particularly through difficult unchartered economic times.

Working capital includes debtors and work in progress balances, but there are other components too which we will cover briefly towards the end of this chapter that include suppliers, unbilled disbursements and taxation reserves. These can also be viewed as a component of working capital in the wider sense, although tax in particular is not covered in specific terms.

First of all we will look at the impact of bad debts on cash flows and profits before considering some of the other important components of working capital control.

The impact of bad debts

Bad debts affect profitability as well as cash flow. Bad debts, expressed as a percentage of fee income, have probably been on average 1 to 2 per cent for professional services firms over the past few years. Some commentators have suggested that this percentage could increase to 4 per cent during the recession. Where firms have a concentration of fee income amongst relatively few clients, and some of these fail, a rate of 5 per cent or higher is not inconceivable.

At the margin, deterioration in collections and higher bad debts has a marked impact on profitability as well as impairing cash flows. Let us take a law firm achieving a 30 per cent net profit margin last year, with bad debts costs at 1 per cent of fee income. The structure of its profit and loss account will be as shown in the middle column of the first scenario shown in Table 7.1. If we then change just the incidence of bad debts as a percentage of fee income, leaving all other costs constant, the impact on equity partner profits is considerable at 10 per cent.

Table 7.1 Scenario 1

Scenario 1	Last Year	Next Year?
Fee income	100%	100%
Bad debts costs	1%	4%
Other costs	69%	69%
Total costs	70%	73%
Profit for equity partners	30%	27%
Percentage reduction in equity partners' profits		10%

Furthermore, it is likely that with decelerating collections, partners will need to wait longer before receiving the balance of their lower profit shares, unless the firm is prepared and able to obtain further borrowings.

In the second scenario shown in Table 7.2 the incidence of bad debts costs is 4 per cent; however, fee income has also fallen by 5 per cent.

Table 7.2 Scenario 2

Scenario 2	Last Year	Next Year?
Fee income	100%	95%
Bad debts costs	1%	4%
Other costs	69%	69%
Total costs	70%	73%
Profit for equity partners	30%	22%
Percentage reduction in equity partners' profits		27%

Partners might not necessarily understand that a reduction in fee income of 5 per cent coupled with worsening debtors' performance will lead to a reduction of over 25 per cent in their profit shares.

It is incumbent on the finance director or accountant to educate partners, and to engage them as fully as possible in the collections process.

Defining the collections process

The collections process needs to be defined clearly. It actually starts with the client opening process and the client care letter, which we set out in Chapter 6. This sets the scene for the bill to be raised to the client. Next it needs to be sent to the client. Then the firm needs to have pre-determined reminder letters or telephone call scripts to follow up with clients. Perhaps a different approach is necessary for corporate and for private clients; however, it is important that all partners understand when the next steps in the credit control process take place, the escalation procedures, the reporting of exceptional performance to the firm's management team, and at what point a letter before action will be sent. It is for the firm's accountant or credit controller to establish the credit control timetable and to highlight problem areas or exceptional items to partners. KPI reporting, as set out Chapter 5, is vital.

Getting partners and fee earners to take action

Behavioural aspects are pivotal. One way to change behaviour is for working capital management to become a component of the appraisal process for partners and for senior lawyers. There needs to be a visible link with performance so that partners with better working capital management generally are more highly remunerated than those with weaker working capital performance.

The role of the finance director or accountant is to set out best practice in working capital, and then motivate the partners and fee earners to achieve, and then maintain this standard. It will certainly be worthwhile in cash flow terms.

The work of the credit controllers is vital; however, the partners have to help them to do their work. Partners need to be encouraged to answer client queries forwarded to them from their credit controller as promptly as they would deal with queries from a prospective new client or an exciting new possible recruit. Those who cancel meetings with the accounts department persistently need to understand that their behaviour has a negative impact on the firm's cash flows. Ideally the firm needs strong management and a 'star chamber' type of system to deal with persistent efforts on the part of partners to delay and avoid their working capital management. The approach needs to be consistent with the culture and style of the firm, but at the end of the day cash flow is the blood of the firm and it therefore needs the appropriate priority.

Utopia

One of the best ways to engage partners in the working capital process is to set out best practice, and what this means for your firm and the impact on your firm's cash flows. Best practice can facilitate:

- payments of prior year profits to partners earlier (particularly if these can be paid before 5 April and invested into their pension or tax efficient savings plans);
- hiring of lateral partners where either strategic or opportunistic;
- not having to be quite so aggressive regarding staff reductions where business processes are already fairly efficient;
- continued investment in new infrastructure;
- less or no reliance upon external bank funding.

There are several ways in which Utopia can be demonstrated to partners. Let us first take debtor days.

If all the firm's clients paid their bills after 30 days, what would be the impact on the firm's cash position, its profit and loss account and its overdraft requirement?

If the percentage of debtors remaining after 90 days reduced to 2 or 3 per cent of the total debtor balance, what would be the impact on cash flows and profits?

Utopia is also used as a tool to improve sluggish billing practices, far too prevalent amongst UK law firms (for whom billing and talking about money with clients is sometimes seen as seedy or undesirable). Why don't you calculate your firm's WIP days and total lock-up days and summarise a few key headlines for your partners, including:

- The impact upon cash flows of reducing firm-wide lock-up to that of the most efficient of your practice areas.
- The impact upon cash flows of reducing firm-wide lock-up to 90 days (in broad terms, 60 days for debtors and 30 days for WIP or 45 days for each).

We believe that the results of these calculations would be startling to most partners.

The hidden debtor days – getting the bill finalised and sending it out to the client

Sadly this is another area where certain fee earners are prone to delays because other parts of their workload are more interesting and intellectually challenging, yet it is absolutely essential for efficient working capital control.

Let us start with a law firm with debtor days of 65 days (ignoring VAT and disbursements). Debtors are £2,000,000 and annual fee income is £11,230,000.

Average daily fees are therefore £30,767. A reduction to say 62 debtor days would reduce debtors by £30,767 × 3 = £92,301.

At the margin, this is probably a sizeable impact on cash flows. Explaining the impact on cash flows of incremental improvements in debtor days to partners is a crucial step in engaging them in the collections process.

To collect a bill it must first of all arrive at the client. Too often bills can be finalised on the firm's accounting system but not actually sent out to clients until several days later. This costs firms money.

Therefore there needs to be very clear responsibility and accountability for the despatch of bills to clients. This should primarily lie with the matter partner or fee earner who approved the bill rather than with the accounts department or with their secretary. In some firms bills are sent out by the accounts department. In others this is the responsibility of partners, in which case the accounts department needs to have clear visibility as to when invoices are actually sent out to clients; a simple invoice register showing the date invoices were finalised and the date they were sent to clients, can work well.

Consider asking your partners to email bills to clients as well as posting them. This avoids them getting 'lost in the post' and they are sent straightaway.

E-billing

Whilst e-billing is only relevant at present for larger law firms, this is something that may become more common over time. E-billing involves a secure and encrypted data file being produced directly from your accounting system which is a rendition of the bill and VAT invoice. This is then validated and uploaded directly to your client's accounts payable system.

After the initial set up and testing phase, e-billing is usually more efficient for both the law firm and its client, and should reduce the time taken to settle the firm's fees.

From a client perspective e-billing can deliver cost savings and more detail on bills, two things which are very attractive to in-house counsel in these times. In a survey of in-house lawyers in **lawgazette.com,** 50 per cent of in-house lawyers wanted to be able to see their bills electronically, and not merely as a PDF copy of the bill in its traditional format.

E-billing therefore brings improved clarity and transparency to the billing process; it also facilitates a fresh dialogue between the firm and its clients about pricing and the use of alternative, more flexible pricing strategies.

Client disputes and working capital

An associated area to look at is client disputes. There needs to be clarity as to who is responsible for dealing with complaints from clients, and it is important to understand how disputes are resolved with clients and how long this takes? The role of the risk partner (or in some cases the senior partner) is key here. Once the profile of client disputes has been identified from a detailed analysis, the risk partner can then improve the underlying risk framework in order to minimise the root causes of these disputes.

It is also important for the finance director to understand patterns emerging from disputes, and how the working capital cycle can be improved to avoid these in future. Often it is a question of clear communication from the outset of a matter to its conclusion. As already discussed, the importance of the client engagement documentation cannot be over-emphasised in its role in working capital management (see Chapter 6).

Managing equity partner retirements and associated cash flows

Increasingly law firms are 'de-equitising' partners, looking at their least profitable practice areas, bringing forward the retirement dates for selected individual partners whose financial contribution is dilutive upon the rest of the firm, and generally being much more businesslike and focused about managing equity partner headcount.

Whilst being desirable in terms of future profit levels and gearing ratios, such actions can cause pain in cash flow terms, at least in the short term.

Clients who are no longer instructing the current firm after their main contact partner has left might be disinclined to settle their remaining bills promptly. Retaining files for work being transferred to another firm where amounts remain unpaid can operate as a lever; however, it is the norm for a letter of undertaking to be provided by the departing partner's new firm. A clear hand-over process is therefore vital for partners leaving the firm with work in progress and debtor balances. In some cases the departing partner's new firm is prepared to purchase work in progress and debtors for migrating clients. In other situations a robust stance with former clients will be necessary, particular if there is no prospect of the old firm being instructed by them in future.

Furthermore, whilst it might be more difficult to collect the recently departed partner's client bills, they are likely to receive additional payments from the firm, including:

- capital and current account balances;
- tax reserves;
- contributions towards their legal expenses;
- additional profit share in their final month with the old firm.

Normally, none of these items will have been budgeted for by the firm's accountant or included within cash flow forecasts. Everything possible therefore needs to be done to match the leaving partners' payments closely to the cash inflows from their remaining working capital. This hidden cost of managing equity partner headcount is often ignored or underestimated. It is therefore incumbent upon the firm's accountant to raise such issues with the managing partner or the Board who will be responsible for taking decisions regarding partner departures.

Working capital and suppliers

It is right to focus on the work in progress and debtors aspects of working capital performance. However, the finance department also needs to pay attention to suppliers and contracts, and squeezing the maximum working capital out of costs. Measures might include considering:

- whether suppliers are paid too early. Making sure that the most favourable credit terms are obtained;
- what payment controls are in place to try to match the outflows with the timing of client collections so as to put minimal strain on the firm's overdraft facility;
- whether payment terms and discounts with suppliers are used to optimise cash. Discounts and rebates and other incentives can have a real impact on cash flows;
- whether all supply and services contracts are properly documented and actively managed;
- whether better value for money could be obtained by putting all substantial supplies and services out to tender every two to three years;
- securing deferred terms for suppliers of recruitment services and similar where the payback in terms of cash generated for the business by the newly arrived partner or fee earner will not take place for some months;
- reviewing terms of business with all suppliers so that there are no unduly onerous clauses for terminating the arrangements with them if the business requires this;
- whether any property leases could be renegotiated in order to free up cash;
- if vacant space could be sublet, or claims made for reductions in business rates;
- reducing the numbers of suppliers through having volume discount arrangements, preferred supplier lists, etc. Suppliers should be willing to offer improved terms, in the same way as clients are exerting pressure on law firms regarding fees and more innovative pricing methodologies. Firms should be as proactive as possible in this area with their key suppliers;
- credit checks that would be run on key suppliers so that in the event of their failure, the firm suffers no loss to its business.

Working capital – at the fringe

There are other aspects of professional services firms' financial management that can have a marked impact on cash flows. The following list is intended as a prompt to ensure that all areas have been addressed and in the quest to strengthen each firm's balance sheet, no stone is left unturned.

- Review defined benefit pension schemes and optimise cash flows through asset for cash swaps, renegotiation of cash payments, etc.
- Optimise tax cash flows including VAT. Maximise VAT reclaims including VAT accruals. Consider salary sacrifice and flexible benefits opportunities to minimise the employers' NI burden.
- The timing of the precise retirement date of an equity partner may be crucial in terms of the associated tax cash flows and should be considered carefully.
- The timing of discretionary expenditure might be varied in order to take best advantage of the change in effective tax rates.
- The interest charges on equity partner borrowings are usually allowable against profits as a qualifying business expense. With the proposed increase in tax rates, it might be possible to amend financing arrangements to secure additional tax relief in 2011–12 on a year's worth of interest.
- If the trend of profits is expected to decline over the next five years then firms may wish to consider changing their accounting date in order to optimise income tax cash flows.

Case study

Provincial High Street firm

How would you describe your firm? (top 100, High Street, publicly funded, etc. ...)	Established 1979 with 2 partners and 2 secretaries. Now approx 90 staff including fee earners. The largest department in numbers and income is the personal injury and clinical negligence department. Clinical negligence work largely publicly funded. Large family department undertaking high proportion of publicly funded work (including public law children work) as well as private work. Growing commercial department, with strategic aim to expand that department further and attract good quality commercial work.
How many partners does your firm have?	6 partners.
How many fee earners (including partners, paralegals and trainees) does your firm have?	Total 41, comprising: 23 personal injury and clinical negligence, 9 family and 9 commercial, property and probate.
What is your position in the firm?	Managing partner
Who is responsible for financial management?	The senior partner is the line manager for the accounts department and has overall responsibility. Managing partner also exercises some responsibility in negotiations with banks and similar matters. Decisions outside the scope or authority of one partner are dealt with either by management executive committee comprising 3 partners, practice manager and office manager, or by full partners meeting.
Could you indicate what action your firm has had to take so far in dealing with the recession?	The hours of the three conveyancers dealing solely with residential conveyancing have been reduced to 4 days or equivalent rather than 5 days. Significant reduction in marketing budget. General economies where possible (e.g. stationery, electricity, gas, etc.). Previously we found ourselves able to pay income tax without resorting to further borrowing, but for January's payment felt it appropriate to borrow for a 6-month term to pay this in order to ease cash flow difficulties. For the first time in the history of the firm, the annual staff pay rise was less than inflation in 2008. No staff have been made redundant, but 2 secretaries who left were not replaced.
Do you have any particular suggestions as to things that have worked in helping your firm adjust?	Certainly, the reduction in salaries and in expenditure on marketing have assisted. It is hoped that the small change in gearing as between fee earners and support staff will help to improve efficiency. It has been important to make staff aware of the need for economies but at the same time avoid spreading alarm and giving any impression that the firm is in difficulties which could so easily lead to staff becoming unsettled and seeking employment elsewhere. 'Steering a steady course' is extremely important.

Were there any ideas that have not worked?	It is difficult to measure some of the smaller savings in stationery and other consumables. We had identified savings which could be made in relation to the library (e.g. unnecessary on-line subscriptions and vast expense of items such as *Halsbury's Statutes* which are little used) but expenditure on library has in fact increased over the year. This is something which is being addressed now.
Do you have any suggestions for managing debtors and WIP?	Each month the accounts department produce for all fee earners (in the family department at least) a list of all privately funded cases on which there is work in progress of more than £250 and fee earners are expected to bill it. The expectation is that money will be obtained on account of costs and that we will cease to work if it is not received or bills not paid. It is very difficult to do this in many family cases in particular and it is a question of trying to equalise the pressure from the client and the pressure to ensure good management of billing. A partner in the department also meets with each fee earner every month to check and review the position with regard to any cases on which there has been no time recorded for a period of 2 months. Every month we review a detailed analysis of debtors, considering all aspects, including the large number of clients who pay by instalments by agreement. Although we had always reserved the right to charge interest, we did not do so until approximately 12 months ago but have now started doing so where appropriate. There is an automatic reminder system set up for the accounts department to submit to the Legal Services Commission claims on account of costs as appropriate at stages after certificates have been issued.
Do you have any suggestions for engaging partners and fee earners and getting them take action to reduce the amounts tied up in working capital?	Different partners in the partnership have different views on this, but my own view is that it is important to share with fee earners some of the financial information such as, for example, the extremely large amount which is outstanding at any one time in disbursements paid but not reclaimed. It is my view that unless fee earners have an idea of the size of the figures, it is difficult for them to realise how much is laid out in disbursements. We also have a procedure whereby if a fee earner is requesting a cheque for a disbursement over £30 for which the money has not been received on account, they are required to complete an 'Emergency Disbursement Slip' justifying paying it out without receiving the money first and confirming that a claim has been submitted to the Legal Services Commission or arrangements made for the client to pay it.
What are the main problem areas you face in making progress?	Changing long-established habits. Getting all fee earners and staff to fully understand the importance of economies and strict financial control. Clients are finding it increasingly difficult to meet legal costs and it is becoming harder to obtain payments on account, when it is at the same time becoming all the more important to do so. In some cases, family cases in particular, it can be very difficult to tell a client we will not act further unless they are able to pay a bill off in full.

What are the main figures you now look at each month to monitor the financial health of the business?	Profit costs received and chargeable hours recorded, by fee earner. Work in progress (when these figures are provided which is not always the case) and realisation rates. The day-to-day cash flow and reconciled office account balance is naturally looked at on a far more frequent basis, almost daily.
For how long do you expect the current recession to last, specifically in terms of the legal sector rather than the economy at large?	Perhaps 18 months to 2 years. There will inevitably be a delay in work returning to the legal sector once the country starts coming out of recession, as it will be some time before clients and prospective clients again gain the confidence (and financial ability) to enter into new business ventures, move house and so on.
Who in your firm is responsible for managing:	
(a) utilisation and fee earner payroll costs;	(a) For (a)–(d) Initially practice manager, but reporting to managing partner, executive and partners' meetings as appropriate.
(b) leverage and secretarial to fee earner and support staff to fee earner ratios;	(b)
(c) support staff payroll costs;	(c)
(d) non-payroll overheads.	(d)
Any other tips?	Most importantly, don't panic! As I have already said, it is important not to spread alarm through the firm but to take prudent and sensible steps and let people see that you are doing so. Avoid making good staff redundant wherever possible as this could fundamentally damage the business and mean that we would be less well placed to increase workloads and workflow when we come out of recession.

Part 3

Positioning the firm to be ready for the upturn

Chapter 8

Strategy post-recession

There will come a point when workflows start to improve, and there are some indications that this has already started for residential property, one of the main areas affected by the recession. Competition is likely to be far stronger after the recession than before, so in order to survive, let alone prosper, firms will need to have become better at planning, better at management and better at being able to spot or create opportunities.

The profession in the UK faced a number of challenges and threats before the recession and these have not gone away. This section considers three of the main issues:

- The Legal Services Act – and what its implications may now be.
- The potential of achieving growth through merger – a live issue for many firms.
- The difficulty of remaining positive and motivating people after all they have been through.

We start by outlining some of the options and the process for developing strategy.

The profession as we come out of recession

By the time the economy starts to recover some firms will:

- be financially weak – they will have limited reserves for investment in new areas;
- have lost some good staff;
- have lost some previously good clients;
- have suffered tensions between the partners, in particular where profits are shared equally;
- have lost their way.

Others will:

- be more focused than before;
- have cut out the 'dead wood';
- have made money even when times were difficult;
- have established much stronger financial systems;
- be doing quite well.

The key, as indicated in the first section is, once your firm's finances are under control, to start planning its recovery. Aim to develop viable and profitable business models that will be sustainable in the long term as the impact of the Legal Services Act start to be felt.

An important element of this will be to develop a positive attitude towards your firm and the opportunities out there. Fiona Westwood develops this later in Chapter 11, but in essence we are talking about:

- an intangible feeling within a firm – you know it when you see it – we can all think of businesses that exude it;
- a 'can do' attitude;
- a belief in yourself, in your people and in your firm;
- it starts from the top and filters down;
- it comes over to others that you deal with – and will make people want to associate themselves with you.

An ability to instil self-belief and positive thinking can have a huge impact on a firm's success.

Size of firm

Whilst there will always be a place for some very small firms, we are likely to see a reduction in the total number of firms and an increase in the average size of each. At the start of the recession nearly 9,000 of the 10,000 or so firms in England and Wales had fewer than four partners, and they probably had fewer than 10 fee earners in all. Work in such firms is generally done by highly experienced, senior solicitors and the standard of work and client care is often high. This type of firm faces a number of challenges:

- Recruitment – the better younger lawyers are often drawn towards the larger firms.
- Succession – the age profile of many of the partners often means that succession will be an issue.
- Long-term profitability – although in the short term they may well generate good profits.
- The difficulty, due to the small number of fee earners to develop effective team structures, through which work can be done at lower cost.

The latter point is especially important because an inabilty to build cost effective teams is central to the long-term difficulties facing many smaller firms. In a typical small firm it is difficult to delegate work to more junior fee earners as very few of these people are employed – the partners are often the primary fee earners. Work tends therefore to be done at a relatively senior level and such work is thus expensive. If a partner is willing to accept very low earnings, or to work very long hours then they are able to undertake work profitably. If however they (correctly) demand reasonable remuneration for the work they put in, and for the risks that they take, then they are expensive people, indeed they are the most expensive people a firm can employ. It will generally not take as long for an experienced person to undertake the work but the true cost of doing that work is still often higher.

Size brings a number of advantages:

- The opportunity for a more profitable practice. As indicated earlier, larger firms, with higher levels of gearing, tend to be more profitable.
- A better ability to deal with succession issues. There are more likely to be prospective partners willing to take over and enter equity.
- A greater ability to recruit as larger firms tend to be more attractive to younger solicitors.
- An ability to develop better financial structures, in particular good levels of gearing, and an ability to develop teams.
- Through team working, the opportunity for work to be done at the appropriate level, so enabling more straightforward work to be undertaken by more junior fee earners at a lower cost, and, where the work is paid on a fixed fee basis, at a higher profit or reduced loss.
- The opportunity to develop areas of specialisation, so enabling the firm to develop a reputation in particular areas of work, and therefore attract better quality business.

- A greater ability to be able to justify the cost of employing support specialists in areas such as IT, finance or HR. IT in particular is becoming ever more important for firms and a larger firm can more easily justify the cost of employing someone to run the system and train and support staff in house. Larger firms can also better afford the finance people who will be ever more important in monitoring the firm's financial performance.

Size also brings a number of drawbacks:

- Larger firms invariably require greater levels of partner capital in order to fund the firm's working capital. In a small firm partner capital could be under £50,000 each. However in a larger firm, with higher levels of gearing, partner capital could easily be £300,000 each. This is because each fee earner carries a certain level of work in progress, unbilled disbursements and debtors, and this will be funded by a combination of borrowings and partner capital. In a larger firm, because there are fewer partners the capital required per partner is greater.
- No firm is easy to manage, but in smaller firms a lack of management often matters less. If most of the fee earners are partners, and if the partners work hard and get on well it is not necessarily a disaster if relatively little real management takes place. Management is never easy in such firms as the firm's administration will often fall on just one of the partners, and that person will have to combine management with fee earning, but in general under-management is not necessarily terminal. Larger firms by contrast are more complicated to manage. Any firm in different buildings or in different towns is a highly complicated business to run. They are complicated mainly by virtue of the larger number of people to manage but they often also require more complicated systems to operate. In a larger firm poor or bad financial management can be disastrous.
- Larger firms, with more non-partner fee earners require more effective systems of supervision.
- Partners in larger firms (should) spend less of their time working with their clients and more of their time supervising staff or trying to generate work. Many partners, in particular those in their 40s or 50s can find this an issue because they went into law to practise as a lawyer. They find their changed role as one of manager or administrator difficult.
- Larger firms often have greater staff turnover.

Options for increased size – organic, merger, or acquisition

There are three main ways of increasing the size of a firm:

- Gradual expansion through recruitment – organic growth.
- Merger with another firm.
- The acquisition or takeover of another firm or team from another firm.

Each approach has its own advantages and disadvantages.

Organic growth

Arguably the best way for any firm to grow is through the selective recruitment of individual people to fill gaps and to allow for the expansion of the practice in line with its overall strategy and the opportunities available to it. Organic growth has a number of advantages:

- It is easier to retain the culture of your practice and its values. In particular, if you recruit people as trainees and train them in your ways and to your standards, it is much easier to maintain the ethos and culture of your firm.
- It is relatively easy to manage. Slow, gradual growth is generally easily absorbed within a firm and does not create a serious management problem. This is not the case of course if a firm is recruiting a number of people simultaneously, although such expansion by definition tends to happen in larger firms that are better able to deal with it.

It also has some disadvantages:

- It is slow – if you are a small firm you might be able to accommodate recruiting an additional fee earner each year, perhaps two. At the same time your larger rivals have added 10 fee earners, perhaps 20.
- There is a real danger that, when you have invested time and energy training someone, they are poached by another firm. Just as they are becoming valuable fee earners you lose them – in particular your good people.

Merger

There are relatively few genuine mergers of equals – most 'mergers' are takeovers and require one firm that is looking to expand through acquisition and another firm willing to be taken over. A merger can:

- create a sudden dramatic expansion and the overnight creation of a much larger practice. Combine two firms each with 30 fee earners and you suddenly create a major player in your town;
- create the opportunity for raising the profile of the combined firm in the market as a whole and for creating relatively strong teams from previously weak ones. They can create depth;
- provide a springboard for expansion.

A genuine merger can however have some downsides:

- Someone needs to take the lead. Any organisation that lacks effective leadership is likely to struggle. Although the merger may start out as a merger of equals someone needs to take a leadership role.
- Simply combining two small firms with poor gearing and low profits can result in a larger firm with poor gearing and low profits. Unless the opportunity is taken to change the financial structure of the combined firm little will have been gained. A merger is a great opportunity for partner retirements. Not everyone will want to be a partner in the new firm – for some approaching retirement this might be the time to leave the partnership, possibly continuing on a consultant basis. It is also an opportunity to re-evaluate the role of an equity partner and for some former equity partners to become salaried in the combined firm. If such financial restructuring does not take place little will have been gained.
- It can be difficult to merge the two cultures. Even where two firms merge into the same building there can be 'rival camps' several years later, in particular amongst support staff. The situation is especially difficult if staff retain the pay and conditions from their previous firms so that in the combined firm staff of the same level are not remunerated in the same way.
- There can be duplication of offices and buildings in locations you do not see as part of your long-term strategy. The problem with a merger is that you take on board the whole firm, and there may be parts you do not want.

- Unless it is agreed that some departments or fee earners will not be included in the merger you might finish up with fee earners and departments you do not want. You might have been attracted by the other firm's litigation team, but you might also acquire a legal aid department that does not fit.
- There may well be incompatibility of IT and telecommunications systems. There can be a temptation to continue parallel systems for a period, which can be confusing and disruptive, and there is always a risk of argument as to which firm's systems should prevail.
- Almost everyone underestimates the management effort required in integrating two law firms, no matter how well intentioned and positive both parties are in principle, and it is important that this does not detract from the fundamental priority of each business, which is their client work.

Acquisition or takeover – of a whole firm or just a team

As indicated earlier, there are relatively few genuine mergers between two equal firms. Most 'mergers' are in reality the takeover of one firm that is weaker, less profitable, may lack strong leadership and management and might have had some bad luck, by one that is stronger. The advantages of growth through acquisition or takeover for the acquiring firm are that:

- The same quantum leap can be achieved as in a merger, but without some of the potential downsides.
- You retain your culture and standards. They are not diluted or compromised.
- If you just take over a team or department you obtain the people you want rather than the 'baggage' that might come with a complete merger.
- If you do have to take over the whole firm you will be in a stronger position to address the weaker or less profitable departments or partners.
- It will be much easier integrating the new people into your systems. They may simply move into your existing offices. Unless the target firm's systems are better, you should be able to introduce your IT systems and ways of working relatively easily.
- It is much easier to improve the acquiring firm's financial structure. Partners may come in but as salaried partners rather than equity.

The advantage for the firm being acquired are that:

- It provides the partners with an exit route. They also should not need to worry about professional indemnity run off cover.
- The partners no longer need to worry about the problems of managing their firm. The larger firm should have the systems and support staff in areas such as IT and finance that they lacked. The partners may well be able to continue on an employed basis acting for their clients, but no longer have to worry about management.
- The fee earners, in particular the younger solicitors, will suddenly have a whole range of career possibilities that may just not have existed in a much smaller firm. It is potentially an exciting time.
- The merger might provide an opportunity for difficult issues, such as an under-performing partner, to be dealt with. Issues that had previously been ignored as being too difficult to deal with may be resolved as part of the merger negotiations.

There are relatively few downsides for the acquiring firm. The main difficulty that might be encountered is that the partners in the target firm may have an inflated view of its value and may expect payment, either in cash or perhaps through a consultancy arrangement in excess of the actual value of the firm. Their expectations can be too high, in particular if they have always viewed the sale of their firm as providing their pension.

The potential disadvantages for the firm being taken over are that:

- The previous partners of the target firm may feel vulnerable to being treated unfairly after they have signed away their independence. There will need to be a well thought through agreement that protects their position.
- The partners might find it difficult to be 'managed' – they will have been used to being the main decision takers in their previous firm and it will probably feel extremely strange to be managed by someone else. Such a situation obviously calls for tact on the part of the acquiring firm.
- Some staff may have difficulty accepting new working conditions and practices. Some long-serving staff may struggle in the new environment and might leave.

The best option?

Arguably there is no ideal scenario, and the needs of each firm will differ; however for many firms, a strategy that combines organic growth with targeted acquisition or takeover is likely to be the most appropriate route. A combined approach will enable the partners to improve their firm's financial structure, in particular its gearing.

The starting points for this process are many, but those that feature very prominently are leadership and effective management, a clear business strategy and reasonably good financial awareness.

Developing strategy

Much has already been written about the process for developing strategy. In essence it is relatively straightforward, and is summarised in Figure 8.1.

Stage one

- Agree an overall 'target market position' for your firm – where you would like it to be in, say, three to five years' time.
- In order to do this you will need to objectively take stock of where you are today, by asking clients, contacts and staff. What do you think is likely to happen in your various markets? How should you respond?
- You should use an external facilitator in order to challenge thinking.
- As part of this you should confirm what your market actually is, in terms of geography, as it may well have changed as a result of the internet and communications. Your market may have been local 10 years ago, but could be national in the future.

Stages two and three

- Develop overall and team or sector plans involving the fee earners in each team.
- Translate these into individual plans for each person.

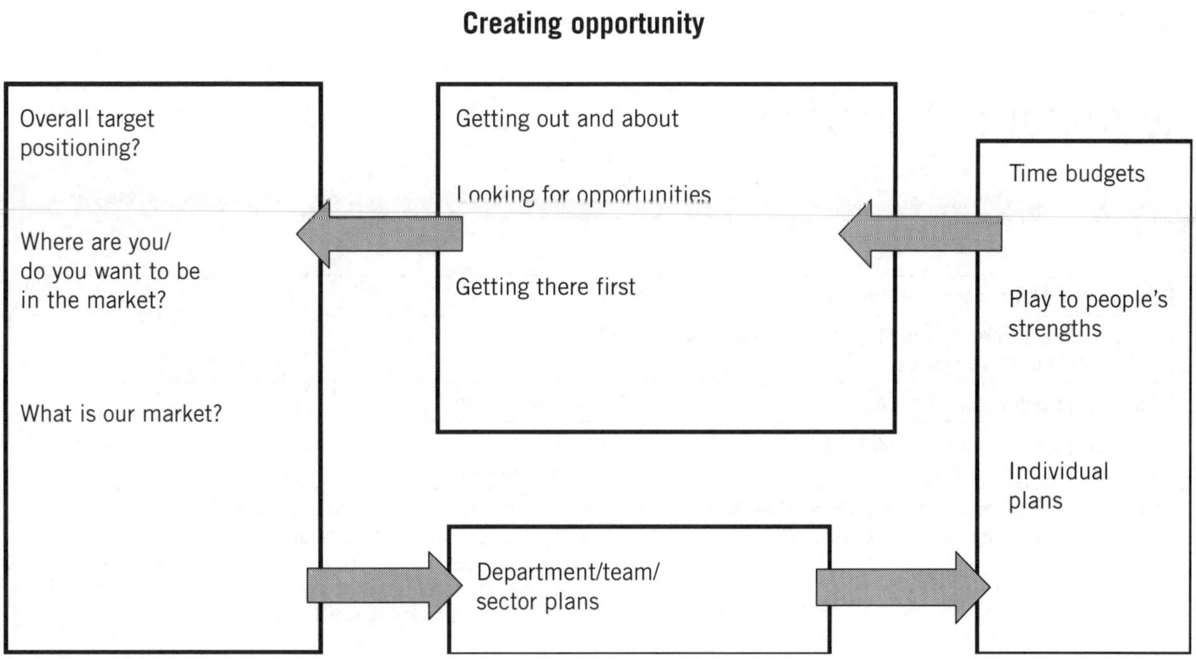

Figure 8.1 Creating opportunity

- Play to each person's strengths.
- Set targets not just for chargeable time but also for non-chargeable areas such as business development and training.

Stage four

- Encourage your people to get out and about as that is when they will stumble across opportunities.
- As always you want to be ahead of other firms, ideally be the only firm.
- You will then be well placed to feed back into the process the following year.

It is also useful to remember that successful firms often:

- find a number of niche areas in which they can excel;
- are good at:
  - managing and motivating people;
  - business development;
  - case management, systems, IT; and
  - the law;
- understand the drivers of law firm profitability;
- achieve a good and consistent standard of client service; and
- are good at developing leadership skills in their people – in particular at team or department head level.

The ideas set out in this chapter were first published in the LMS Legal Aid Toolkit.

Case study

Regional full service

How many partners does your firm have?	21
How many fee earners (including partners, paralegals and trainees) does your firm have?	58
What is your position in the firm?	Managing partner
Who is responsible for financial management?	The buck stops here, but all the clever stuff is done by our finance manager.
Could you indicate what action your firm has had to take so far in dealing with the recession?	Most if not all of the things you've heard other firms try: redundancies, reduced hours/pay, redeployment, salary freezes & cuts, etc., etc. The aim throughout has been to retain all key staff so as to maintain service levels and be ready to take advantage of the upturn as and when it comes.
Do you have any particular suggestions as to things that have worked in helping your firm adjust?	Communication – we have been open, honest and timely in all our communications with our staff about the firm's financial performance. When bad news has had to be delivered it has never been a surprise. Our staff have shown a reasoned understanding of all the measures we have implemented, and their ongoing commitment and loyalty has been one of the real pluses for us this year.
Were there any ideas that have not worked?	Not knowing how long nor how deep the recession was going to be (I still don't!) meant that some steps in 2008 weren't as big and bold as they could/should have been. So one very small redundancy round inevitably led to another; and one small reduction in partner drawings only delayed a larger cut later.
Do you have any suggestions for managing debtors and WIP?	All our departments are targeted for lock-up reduction by reference to the top quartile figures published in the LMS Financial Benchmarking Survey. In some departments, individuals have annual lock-up targets. We publish lock-up figures by department to all staff.
Do you have any suggestions for engaging partners and fee earners and getting them take action to reduce the amounts tied up in working capital?	Peer group pressure seems to work for us. The firm's lock-up has reduced in just over 2 years from 226 days to 166. We are now aiming to get below 150 days.
What are the main problem areas you face in making progress?	Striking the right balance (in the face of my partners' wildly differing opinions) in decision-making for the short, medium and long-term future of the firm. Persuading the shareholders to let managers manage.
What are the main figures you now look at each month to monitor the financial health of the business?	Cash flow, fees billed, time captured and lock-up, in that order!
For how long do you expect the current recession to last, specifically in terms of the legal sector rather than the economy at large?	Until at least Spring 2010.

Who in your firm is responsible for managing:	
(a) utilisation and fee earner payroll costs;	(a) Department managers (DMs) are responsible for managing utilisation in their departments; fee earner payroll costs are to a degree within their remit too, but with input from our finance manager and myself
(b) leverage and secretarial to fee earner and support staff to fee earner ratios;	(b) Again this will be something discussed and agreed between DMs and finance/myself
(c) support staff payroll costs;	(c) Another three-way conversation: our business manager, the finance manager and me
(d) non-payroll overheads.	(d) Same as (c)
Any other tips?	Regular trips to the Lake District help, and between those I rely on friends, family, red wine and painkillers ...

Chapter 9

Implications and opportunities post-Clementi?

Simon Young[1]

Timing of the Legal Services Act's introduction

The Legal Services Act 2007 (the Act) was passed into law at the very end of that year, at a time when the financial problems which were about to hit the legal profession, and its marketplace, were undreamt of. Its underlying philosophy was founded on the proposition that the demand for legal services would continue to grow, and that it was the consumers of those services – whether corporate or personal – whose interests had to be protected.

It was however always envisaged that the implementation of the Act would take some years to achieve, not least because it required the establishment of a number of new bodies who would be responsible for its operation. It has therefore followed the pattern of modern legislation, with a series of Commencement Orders bringing different parts of the Act into force at different times. It is not expected that it will be fully in force until 2011 at the earliest.

In terms of the business structures which the Act is to permit, there are two key stages. The first was at 31 March 2009, when the two forms of legal disciplinary practice (LDP) which are outlined below became possibilities. The latter had been thought likely to be in 2012, but the Legal Services Board (LSB), the overarching regulator created by the Act, now says it wants to achieve this by 2011. That latter stage will be the creation of alternative business structures (ABSs), which may or may not also be multi-disciplinary practices (MDPs).

It follows, therefore, that between the passing of the Act, and the implementation of its first commercially important stage, the level and profitability of legal business have suffered considerably. How then has that affected the attractions or drawbacks of the Act?

Understanding some of the terms in the Act

The key to understanding LDPs is to know some of the language of the Act. It talks about 'reserved legal activities', which can only be performed by those who are authorised by the Act to do so. The extent of those activities may be altered by the LSB, but at present they are:

- the exercise of a right of audience;
- the conduct of litigation;
- reserved instrument activities;
- probate activities;

1 Simon Young, MBA, Solicitor, Founder Member of Law Consultancy Network.

- notarial activities; and
- the administration of oaths.

The term for lawyers is thus coined in reference to those activities and they are referred to as 'authorised persons'. There are eight different kinds:

- solicitors;
- barristers;
- legal executives;
- licensed conveyancers;
- notaries public;
- trade mark agents;
- patent agents; and
- costs draftsmen.

No one type of authorised person can undertake all the reserved legal activities, and some may be very limited, e.g. costs draftsmen.

The third term which it is necessary to understand is a confusing one, because it does not mean what it says. The Act uses the term 'manager' to refer to:

- a partner in a general partnership;
- a member of a limited liability partnership (LLP); and
- a director in a limited company.

Such a person does not, however, have to manage at all. The Act merely assumes that, because of their position, they are entitled to manage.

Understanding legal disciplinary practices

Once those terms are understood, it is possible to move on to understand what is meant by a legal disciplinary practice or LDP. The first thing to note, which applies to all LDPs, is that they are still limited as to the services which they can offer. So, if an LDP wants to offer any services which are outside the normal scope of legal services, it will have to satisfy the same tests as a normal solicitors' firm (see rule 21 of the Solicitors' Code of Conduct 2007).

The basic idea of an LDP is that the body of owners of the business – the 'managers' – may come from a wider range of backgrounds than before. This can be achieved in one of two ways. First, there may be a mix of managers who are authorised persons, so that, for instance, the partners in a firm might be a mixture of solicitors, barristers, legal executives and licensed conveyancers. This ought to be easy – in regulatory terms – to achieve. No permissions are needed, and those bringing in new blood merely need to check the professional qualifications of those who have agreed to join them.

Nonetheless, there may be vestigial problems from previous professional regulations, which need to be relaxed, but have not yet been. So, for instance, for practising barristers to join in partnership with solicitors, the regulators of the Bar need to relax the rule which says that barristers cannot practise in partnership. At the time of writing, they have not yet done so, and it is understood that they intend to deal with initial moves by way of individual waivers. This is against the spirit of the Act, which envisages no obstacles to such moves.

The second way of achieving an LDP is, however, more complex. This is the idea that those who are not lawyers at all may become managers in the business – in the special sense of manager mentioned above. Here, there are more restrictions. The nature of those restrictions will depend upon the regulator which is ultimately responsible for the business. As an illustration, take the Law Society, as authorised regulator, operating through the Solicitors Regulation Authority (SRA). If a firm of solicitors wishes, for instance, to appoint its non-lawyer chief executive as a partner, it has to apply to the SRA for a declaration that the applicant is a suitable person.

Further, the number of such non-lawyers, and the extent of their ownership and control of the business, are strictly limited. Briefly, for a solicitors' firm, there have to be at least three authorised persons (lawyers from whatever branch of the profession) for each non-authorised person; and at least 75 per cent of the ownership and control of the firm must remain in lawyers' hands. Note that these precise conditions apply to solicitors' firms. There are conditions that attach to other sorts of business, which are of the same broad nature, but not the same in their application. Thus, a licensed conveyancers' firm will fulfil its requirements if at least one manager is a licensed conveyancer, regardless of the number and level of interest of other managers.

There are two more features of this half of the LDP regime, which may both be off-putting. One is that if a firm is close to the margins of compliance with the above conditions, an event beyond its control can render it non-compliant, and the requirements for getting back on track are stringent. Imagine a firm with three lawyers as partners, and one non-lawyer, where one of the lawyers suddenly dies. The death makes the firm non-compliant, and the only ways in which it can restore compliance are either to appoint another lawyer, or to remove the non-lawyer. The rules give only a month for one or other of these drastic steps to be taken.

The other is that the rules which govern this half of the LDP regime are only temporary. When the rules governing ABSs come into force (approx 2011) then any legal services firm which wants non-lawyer participation in its ownership will become an ABS – a 'licensable body' in the language of the Act – and will have to apply for a licence to operate as such. Since the rules for ABSs are as yet a long way off, it follows that firms may be deterred from committing themselves to a structure which, in perhaps only two years' time, will be under a different, and as yet unknown, regulatory regime from the already complex one which exists at present.

As mentioned, this new regime has been introduced against a background of drastic economic change. What effect has that had? For a start, it is likely to have put members of an already largely conservative profession off any move which smacks of innovation and departure from accepted norms. In a time when survival is the watchword, it is difficult for even the far-sighted to persuade themselves that in fact the best way of beating the increasingly fierce competition in a shrinking marketplace might well just be the sort of differentiation which LDPs offer as an opportunity.

Also, it may be that it is just the sort of legal business which might otherwise have been thinking along LDP lines that may have suffered most. Those businesses which are heavily committed to 'commoditised' services – delivered through dedicated centres, with highly intensive IT usage and high ratios of unqualified staff, serving a mass consumer market, e.g. residential conveyancing and re-mortgaging, have seen their fortunes drastically worsen. In more normal climes, businesses of that modernised model might have been seen as the most likely to use cross-disciplinary inputs and professional management.

Further, looking at the position from the perspective of the proposed incomer, the crude question must be – what's in it for me, as against the risk to me? Many firms already have senior management who are handsomely remunerated, often on a par with partners. Those individuals, however, are free from personal risk. Why then should they – for no or little extra reward – take on an element of personal risk? This is clearly less of a problem in a limited liability environment, e.g. if the business is an LLP or company, but it will nonetheless come into any incomer's thinking.

The result of all this was that, immediately before the LDP regime came into force, the SRA announced that it had had only 14 advance applications for certification of 'suitable' persons wishing to come into the sector of LDPs which will mix lawyer and non-lawyer managers. (There is as yet no comparable statistic for the other half of LDPs, which merely mix different sorts of lawyer, as no permissions are needed there, and the only obligation is to notify the SRA. Such figures will emerge over time.)

So, are LDPs a waste of time? Not necessarily. The next section will therefore look at what opportunities may be presented by this new business model.

Business advantages of LDPs

Where then may LDPs offer positive advantages for legal businesses? Consider first the type of LDP which is mixing lawyers from different backgrounds. This might be used to gain market presence in an area of work which is already a specialism, by integrating different tiers of work. So, for instance, a litigation business might benefit from a mixture of:

- barristers, offering both research capabilities and specialist knowledge on the one hand, and advocacy skills on the other;
- solicitors, responsible for marketing the business and managing it;
- legal executives, managing and carrying out the casework.

This model could be brought about in a number of different ways. An obvious one would be for an existing solicitors' firm to take in a number of barristers from a local chambers, thus not only securing their expertise but denying it to neighbouring competitor firms who would otherwise have briefed those barristers. (Or, alternatively, supplying the expertise as a firm to those competitors.) It is however also a matter of record that a number of barristers' chambers have declared their interest, in principle, in taking over a firm of solicitors, in order to secure a flow of properly managed work. The increases in overall size resulting from such moves may well be seen as offering increased opportunities for access to traditional sources of capital (principals and banks) which smaller firms may find difficult in current climes.

This principle could be used either to gain market share in a particular marketplace, or alternatively to diversify the services on offer. Lateral hire of partners, to break into a new area of work, is a well-trodden path, but is always a difficult move, and one aspect which usually needs considering is the restrictive covenants which may bind the incomer. If however that incomer is a barrister then by definition he will not be subject to any such covenants. Further, the addition of this sort of opportunity serves to broaden substantially the pool from which proposed lateral hires can be drawn.

Another possibility of LDPs may be to allow a business to do some 'regulator-shopping', in order to select a regulatory regime of a less burdensome nature. For instance, solicitors have often wished to be able to operate their conveyancing businesses under the rules applicable to licensed conveyancers, as they are seen as less restrictive, e.g. in relation to acting on both sides of a matter. Previously, solicitors have not been able to take a share in the ownership of a licensed conveyancers' business without surrendering their practising certificates. That will no longer be the case. So, a solicitors' practice would be able to hive off its conveyancing business into a separate entity (preferably an LLP or a company) in which they could openly have an interest, but which would not be subject to SRA regulation.

Turning to the introduction of non-lawyers as owners, this may offer increased possibilities of strengthening the management of the firm. Subject to the point as to risk mentioned above, it may well be advantageous for a firm to be capable of incentivising its senior management by offering the status of principals. This may also help to overcome the 'them and us' mentality which still prevails in all too many law firms when management's status is considered. Once lawyers accept that their management colleagues share on like terms to them, they may be more prepared to allow those colleagues to do their job, and manage the firm properly without interference. Since, as will be seen later in this chapter, efficient and professional management is seen as essential for any business aspiring to ABS status, it may well be that this move offers an interim opportunity to embed superior management in the firm prior to 2011.

There will however undoubtedly be difficulties in introducing new partners, etc. from different backgrounds. This work does not deal with the ethical and regulatory aspects, but even in straight economic terms there are many questions to be determined. For instance, solicitors will normally have a higher level of capital invested per head in their businesses than barristers; whereas barristers will be used to remuneration packages which are much more related to the 'eat what you kill' philosophy, and yield much higher margins, than the collective concept of lockstep, and the lower overall margins of solicitors' operations. These are issues which will need to be dealt with sensitively if the changes are to stick, to the satisfaction of all.

Alternative business structures – the split of ownership, management and delivery

A more fundamental change will be with us in two or three years' time, namely the introduction of alternative business structures (ABSs). Known technically as 'licensable bodies', these will be any business which wishes to deliver legal services – whether or not it also offers other services – which is not entirely within the ownership of lawyers. In other words, as soon as you have a mixture of lawyers and others in a legal business, you have an ABS, and that is why any existing LDPs which have non-lawyer managers will become ABSs. In such bodies, though the actual client-facing delivery of legal services will remain the responsibility of lawyers, they may play little or no part in the ownership and/or the management of the business.

The granting of licences for ABSs will be in the hands of 'licensing authorities'. There are likely to be very few of these. The Law Society/SRA will be seeking the sanction of the LSB to act in this capacity, but the Bar Council will not. It remains to be seen what the attitude of other regulators will be. In considering whether or not to grant a licence, the authority will need to consider, amongst other things, the effect of such a grant on 'access to justice'. Unfortunately, that latter phrase is not defined, and different interpretations may give rise to difficulty.

Essentially, any fit and proper person, certified as such by an appropriate licensing authority, will be able to own a part of a business which offers legal services. The stringency of the tests which an applicant has to pass may increase with the share held, but the default position is that a 10 per cent holding is enough to trigger the requirement. It follows therefore that, unless application is made to a licensing authority which has chosen a lower threshold, a person could acquire, say, a 5 per cent stake in a business without needing to pass any tests. Authorities will have the power to say that no individual may have more than a set percentage of the ownership; and also that the aggregate of non-lawyer holdings must not exceed a percentage. If those powers are exercised, then the possibility of a legal business entirely owned by non-lawyers is not a foregone conclusion.

What then will be the attraction of ABSs? From the perspective of an existing firm, they may offer additional access to capital. In a profession whose businesses are often under-capitalised, this may prove attractive. It was said that the likes of the 'Magic Circle' firms would not be interested as they had sufficient capital anyway: whether that same view will prevail in the era after recessionary calls upon partners for very substantial cash injections is another matter. It is worth remembering, in the context of the banking and financial services industries, that a great many of the household names whose fortunes – or misfortunes – have been much in evidence in the media in 2008 and 2009 were, until fairly recent times, partnerships wholly in the hands of the relevant professionals. It seems that the lure of external capital may be hard to resist.

External capital may be achieved by a number of routes, but the two most likely will be full or partial flotation on a stock exchange, or the injection of capital from private venture firms. Flotation has been tried by one firm in New South Wales, with reasonable success, but the fact that it has not yet been replicated in that jurisdiction means that it may not be seen as the answer to all prayers. It may particularly suit one business model, which is that used in the accountancy profession by companies such as Numerica and Tenon, namely an accumulation by takeover of small firms, to build a large one.

One thing which will be common to any such form of opening up of ownership will be the desire of the new owners for first class management. They are likely only to approach firms they already consider to be well managed, but they will want to have their own management input, bringing in the experience of managers in the broader sectors of industry than lawyer-managers will have experienced. In particular, if the firm is to be a multi-disciplinary practice (MDP) then the managerial tasks of coordinating a diverse business with participants from different professional and cultural backgrounds, and a range of services, will present a major management challenge.

So the lawyers in a business, from being owners/managers/deliverers, may shrink to the latter status only. Clearly, they will only wish to suffer this change if there is sufficient reward, in terms of capital to be received and withdrawn by them. In other words, they will be swapping traditional business models, which are good at generating good profit margins, but yield little capital reward, for a model where they release capital but see a diminution in subsequent income.

From the investors' viewpoint, they will need to know that the business is going to be capable of sustainably yielding what may be termed 'superprofits'. The profits of any business can be conceptually divided, though this is something which lawyers often omit to do. With any normal form of investment, one of the chief characteristics which will sway an investor is return on capital. Lawyers, however, often invest hundreds of thousands of pounds in their firms, without ever considering whether they are getting an adequate return for this element of their involvement. The second element is reward for their hands-on involvement as a lawyer – the equivalent of a salary. The third element is a reward for the risk which they are taking. A firm will only deliver superprofits if it regularly produces more than a reasonable aggregate for these three forms of profit. Only if there is sufficient after paying such constituent elements as may still be appropriate for the lawyers will there be any return for the investors.

Commercial impact of ABSs

Where then may be the expected areas of actual commercial impact of ABSs? It is not sufficient for small firms to say that the new models will not affect them, as they will not be likely to attract external investment. The point is that their competition may well come from such firms. At the top, commercial, end of the market, there may be external investment in existing major firms, which will not affect High Street firms. That is not, however, the only likely manifestation of the new possibilities.

The model of the commoditised firm may be tarnished in the light of the failure of some conveyancing businesses; but that is not to say it does not remain attractive in principle. The lesson to be learned from those difficulties is that over-concentration on a limited range of suppliers, and a limited range of products, offers scant protection when market conditions change. It does not alter the basic truth that some legal services can be delivered from a business which relies heavily on unadmitted (but well-supervised) staff, and heavy IT involvement. There are still a number of such businesses which are thriving, and which are now seeking to adapt the skills they have honed in delivering low cost services in particular sectors, so they can apply them to other types of work.

This is likely to prove attractive to external businesses, and already they are queuing up. The likes of the Co-operative Legal Services already use the provisions relating to the delivery of services by in-house solicitors to facilitate the provision of services to the millions of members they have. They have the infrastructure all ready to roll out those services, in carefully chosen sectors, to the general public. Another model is a flatter structure, funded by loan capital and not therefore needing to satisfy a large number of partners, which concentrates on bulk work involving consumers, but where the consumer is the other party, such as mortgage repossession work.

The key is going to be the ability to gain access to the marketplace with a reasonably priced offering. One way of achieving this is already being seen, with internet-based chains of firms. The organisers seek no involvement in the firms, but ask for payment of subscriptions for net-based marketing, in return for offering instructions from those attracted by the marketing. One logical development of this quasi-franchising approach, however, is likely to be a need to be able to certify the quality of service offered, and hence an element of control of firms' systems by the central company.

Further, the multi-disciplinary aspects of ABSs should not be ignored at High Street level. There seems to be an assumption that mixing different disciplines will be the prerogative of large firms only. Certainly some are likely to go down this route. The major firms which are thought of as accountants are often not any longer 'chartered accountants', as too high a proportion of their members come from other professional disciplines to allow them to continue to use that nomenclature. Their previous relative lack of success with ventures into 'associations' with law firms – tried and abandoned by several – may put them off, but inevitably some will conclude that that was the result of a more restrictive regulatory regime, and that the fundamental idea of combination should be taken out again and dusted off.

It will however be open to all firms to consider whether increasing the range of their services will give them the greater market positioning and access that they will need to compete. What if, for instance, a solicitors' practice merges with, or takes over, the estate agents on one side and the accountants on the other? Yes, there will be regulatory issues, but any barriers should not be impossible to cross. There should be unitary cost savings (e.g. none of the three firms could afford a full-time compliance officer, but they can easily absorb a third of the costs of one), and there should be both increased market share in terms of overall professional services, as well as possibly increased access to traditional forms of capital from sheer size.

Such combinations could be either broad brush, as in the last paragraph, or they could be client-focused. Imagine, for instance, a law firm with a good client base in the property development area. Even though these are not good times for that area, that may mean this is a good time to be planning for what happens when there is the inevitable upturn. Say the firm also has good planning strengths. Why should it not look to recruit, perhaps as participants in a hived-off unit, surveyors, architects, town planners and plot sales agents, so as to offer their developer clients a one-stop service for all their professional needs?

Structuring the business

The last paragraph referred in passing to one of the key questions which any law firm is going to need to address in the new era, namely, what is the right structure and legal vehicle for it. The possibilities can be summed up in the matrix below:

	Partnership	Limited liability partnership	Limited company
Status quo	X	X	X
LDP – lawyers only	X	X	X
LDP – inc non-lawyers	X	X	X
ABS – legal services only	X	X	X
ABS – range of services	X	X	X

There is nothing in regulatory terms to require a firm to move away from the top left-hand corner if they wish. In other words, if they believe their future is best faced as a traditional partnership, with solicitor-only ownership, that is fine. There are however other pressures which may serve to suggest that moves down and to the right may be desirable.

On the one hand there is the element of risk, which must logically incline managers to an LLP or company structure. The risk in question is not merely the risk of negligence claims, upon which some solicitors' minds can be unduly set. After all, such claims are compulsorily insured, and firms should by now, with the impact of Lexcel and rule 5 of the Solicitors' Code of Conduct 2007 in particular, have designed their systems to minimise such risk. Risks with much more danger are surely those which are by nature both unpredictable and uninsured, such as discrimination claims; and those which are contractual rather than tortious, namely straightforward trading losses – seen recently in many firms.

The other element however is that of the competitive positioning of the firm. What competition will it face, with its position in the various marketplaces it inhabits, i.e. the geographic area it is based in, the price range it chooses, the nature of the services it delivers, etc.? And how best will it face that competition, according to the business model it chooses?

Again, it seems likely that one or other corporate model may have advantages. First, as mentioned in Chapter 3, such entities will be likely to need properly audited accounts, which will be a great comfort to would-be investors. Second, the corporate bases will be much more flexible, particularly if there is to be a range of business operations within one overall umbrella operation – a model which may appeal to many. Third, external investors will be more comfortable with vehicles they are used to. Fourth, companies may have the edge in terms of their use for staff incentivisation through share bonus schemes, though the attractions of this may have been weakened by the bonus scheme scandals in the banking industry, and the illustration they have offered that focusing on the wrong aims can be disastrous. Finally, and by way of introduction to the next chapter, if merger is sought by firms to increase their resilience, then such mergers will be easier to achieve through the use of corporate structures than in partnership. Change may therefore not be obligatory or inevitable, but it does seem to have a lot going for it.

Case study

Specialist criminal law practice

How many partners does your firm have?	4 equity and 2 salaried
How many fee earners (including partners, paralegals and trainees) does your firm have?	15
What is your position in the firm?	Managing and senior partner
Who is responsible for financial management?	Me!
Could you indicate what action your firm has had to take so far in dealing with the recession?	As a legal aid practice costs are closely monitored and kept to a minimum – as such the recession has had no effect. Our raw materials are criminal cases which tend to increase during times of financial difficulty.
Do you have any particular suggestions as to things that have worked in helping your firm adjust?	Watching every penny and being able to cover all areas of criminal law are the key (i.e. having a VHCC contract, opening a prison law department, increasing use of solicitor advocates) to maximising the workload. Taking opportunities when they arise, for example opening an office in nearby town when other firms are withdrawing from legal aid work and attracting the right people.
Were there any ideas that have not worked?	Not so far!
Do you have any suggestions for managing debtors and WIP?	We have no bad debt. We operate without a client account and only undertake private client work once we have payment in advance. WIP is easier to manage in a legal aid firm.
What are the main problem areas you face in making progress?	Our main problems are external – the changes envisaged to legal aid in the future and the political decisions over which we have no control.
What are the main figures you now look at each month to monitor the financial health of the business?	I look at the figures every day! Most importantly: • the reconciliation with the standard monthly payment as it is our bread and butter • expenditure/outlays • profit and loss accounts.
For how long do you expect the current recession to last, specifically in terms of the legal sector rather than the economy at large?	2–3 years
Who in your firm is responsible for managing:	
(a) utilisation and fee earner payroll costs;	(a) Managing partner and cashier
(b) leverage and secretarial to fee earner and support staff to fee earner ratios;	(b) Managing partner
(c) support staff payroll costs;	(c) Cashier
(d) non-payroll overheads.	(d) Managing partner and cashier

Chapter 10

Merger as part of your strategy?

Colin FitzPatrick[1]

Identifying the issues

Mergers should arise out of a strategic business decision rather than a long acquaintance between partners of the different firms or merely out of a desire to be bigger on the grounds that it would look better to be bigger. It is perfectly reasonable to feel that a merger is needed for self-preservation or defensive reasons, as well as for more positive or aggressive reasons, but those motives in themselves are business-driven. Business is about earning profits, albeit in accordance with certain standards of behaviour.

On the basis that the decision to seek a merger partner is a business transaction, the process should be conducted in a formal and businesslike manner, and should at all times be regarded as a 'negotiation' rather than 'clubbing together', on the basis that others in a firm will follow the lead of the partners, and the image that is projected will set the tone of the new firm.

Identifying a merger candidate is not necessarily an easy process. It assumes first that a candidate is available, and secondly that the candidate is willing to talk. The initial approach is therefore essential. However, preceding this, there needs to be an internal analysis by the seeking firm to identify the candidate. A picture of the ideal merger partner should be drawn up without reference to any specific firm, and then firms in the requisite area should be matched with the pre-developed criteria. This is a form of 'Dutch' selection process, as all enquiries will have to be made without the knowledge of the candidates.

Once a potential merger candidate has been identified, the method of approach should be determined. This is usually best done 'senior partner to senior partner', preferably at a meeting, although this will invariably be prefaced with a telephone conversation. Nothing should be in writing at this stage. The initiating firm should have a list of reasons to go through with the potential merger candidate, once the idea that the candidate would consider a merger has been determined in principle. It may be that the merger candidate has other plans, or it is not at the point that it considers a merger to be feasible; however, most firms will not reject the idea out of hand and will want to hear the reasons why it is felt that a merger would be mutually beneficial. It is possible that the initial meeting would include around three partners from each firm or that a subsequent meeting with several or all of the partners is held before it is decided that merger discussions should begin.

Once a decision to hold initial merger discussions has been agreed, an early decision should be made on whether to utilise an independent facilitator or project manager, as a form of non-executive chair and/or a driver of the requisite actions. This can assist in getting things going, identifying issues, dealing with them and keeping things going. These responsibilities can be

1 Colin FitzPatrick is a Principal with FitzPatrickRoyle.

undertaken by appointed partners, but a facilitator can minimise partners' time commitment to the merger and allow them to keep their 'eye on the ball' as far as the business is concerned, as well as retain a position where they are able to 'see the woods for the trees'. Professional advisers could be used to move the process along, but there can be conflicts as well as cost inefficiencies in doubling-up their involvement.

If he or she is a non-executive chair, the facilitator must be trusted by both parties, regarded as independent and having the interests of the potential merged firm in mind rather than any individual interests. This kind of person can be difficult to find, but if one is available, then he or she should be seriously considered. A project manager is more of a consultant who would carry out specific tasks, which may culminate in the physical moving of people, IT and files.

The first meeting, as with first impressions, can be the most important in setting the tone in the negotiations and merger process. The parties should be properly prepared and the meeting should be structured.

The meeting should be treated with a certain amount of caution, assuming that a decision has not yet definitely been made to proceed with a merger. It would not be appropriate to part with too much information until a definite decision has been made to proceed with detailed negotiations. Furthermore, enthusiasm should be controlled to keep one's negotiating strength intact. It is at this stage that confidentiality agreements can be agreed and signed.

The initiative can largely be retained by demonstrating meticulous preparation at every stage of negotiation and limiting the first meeting to establishing information on points of principle that could be deal breakers or, at least, determine whether or not detailed negotiations should take place. However well the first meeting goes, it would be a mistake to allow that meeting to drift into detailed discussions.

Following the first meeting, and on the basis that a decision is taken to proceed with negotiations, you should consider a detailed checklist encompassing more than 100 questions or topics that need to be investigated, along with guidance on other steps to be taken.

Developing the structure for moving forward

As stated before, the first meeting is often the most important in setting the tone during negotiations and the merger process. The parties should be properly prepared, and the meeting should be structured. Some items that should appear on a potential first meeting agenda include:

- opening statements on the potential advantages and disadvantages of a merger;
- respective work ethics/philosophies of the partnerships;
- development plans of both partnerships before the merger idea arose;
- policies of both partnerships on such issues as capitalisation, profit sharing, distribution policy and drawings arrangements;
- exchange of financial indicators and discussion thereof;
- major clients and potential conflicts of interest;
- legal issues (contracts, obligations and claims);
- premises;
- possible name of merged firm;
- personnel responsible for handling the negotiations; and
- outline timetable.

Each side should state what it sees as the purpose of the merger, the perceived advantages and potential disadvantages.

At an early stage, the respective partnership philosophies and compatibility need to be put to a preliminary test. For this purpose, the following should be discussed at the initial meeting:

- the respective work ethics of both partnerships;
- the development plans of both partnerships before the merger idea arose; and
- the policies of both partnerships on such issues as capitalisation, profit sharing, distribution policy and drawings arrangements.

Limited financial indicators could be exchanged to ensure no great disparities exist in performance or aspirations. Table 10.1 requires information to provide a general comparative financial picture, without revealing detailed accounts.

Table 10.1 Initial comparator information to be exchanged

	Firm A	**Firm B**
	y/e	y/e
Total fees	£	£
Staff costs	£	£
Staff costs as % of fees	%	%
Number equity partners (EPs) in year		
Staff costs including EPs' salary £50k	£	£
Staff costs as % of fees including EPs'	%	%
Other overheads as % of fees	%	%
Equity profit as % of fees	%	%
Equity profit as % of fees after EPs' salaries	%	%
Average profit per EP	£	£
Total partnership capital/current accounts (excluding tax reserve)	£	£
Total partnership capital/current accounts (including tax reserve)	£	£
Accounts work in progress (WIP)	£	£
WIP as % of fees	%	%
Bank indebtedness	£	£

Without providing full client listings, it would be prudent to discuss each firm's major clients and their likely reaction to a merger. Also, it would be useful to examine any potential major conflicts of interest that could be so important as to raise a question over taking things further.

Although a number of legal issues may eventually need to be looked at carefully, the initial meeting should be used to seek information on certain primary issues suggested below and, if not immediately available, at least request from each other information on the following:

- details of all material, contractual obligations of the other firm, including such matters as property leases, leases of equipment, hire-purchases and the like;
- obligations to retired partners and/or their dependants;
- any pending lawsuits against the firm;

- any past lawsuits against the firm or any individual partner;
- any known circumstances that could give rise to such claims; and
- any HM Customs and Revenue enquiries into the firm and/or partners.

It would be useful to have an initial discussion with regard to the likely position regarding premises, should the merger proceed, in particular, such matters as the following.

- Will existing premises be adequate and/or appropriate for the merged firm?
- Will consolidation in one location be possible, thereby giving rise to economies of scale?
- If so, how disposable are premises that might become redundant, or would there be ongoing obligations?
- If new premises will be necessary, are these economically viable and obtainable?

Even at the first meeting, the matter of the name of the merged firm should be raised, at least to discover whether and to what extent agreeing upon a name will create problems. Some mergers have floundered because name agreement could not be reached when it had been left until too late in negotiations to be resolved.

Should the meeting agenda items be covered in a broadly satisfactory manner without raising seemingly insurmountable problems, then the meeting can be concluded on the basis that the partners will retrench and consider whether they wish to take negotiations further, or they can decide then and there that they should deal immediately with three further items:

- decide who, from both sides, will handle detailed negotiations, either in liaison with a facilitator or in tandem;
- create a policy regarding information exchange and security arrangements during negotiations; and
- appoint a 'PR person' in each firm and make arrangements within both firms so that, should a leak or something arise that results in an employee or client asking a question, or a call from the press, regarding the potential merger, then the issue or enquiry will be directed to the designated individual or individuals. It is prudent to legislate for this at the beginning, as it should help avoid generating confusion that could give rise to potentially damaging rumours.

Understanding the financial indicators

This section relates to the financial indicators set out above and their relevance and potential significance to a merger. General indicators can be broken down into more detail in due course.

Total fees in themselves are not a safe indicator, as it is efficiency and profitability that are important. However, all other things being equal, fees should be an indicator of the relative sizes of the firms, and potentially of the merged firm, which enables comparison with other similar-sized firms if information is available.

Staff costs as a percentage of fees are an indicator of efficiency and profitability, albeit that the gearing of partners can distort the ratio, which is why it is advisable to also carry out a calculation that imputes a notional salary per equity partner. The level of this notional salary is debatable and depends on the size and earning capacity of the business and partner expectations. The appropriate figure is likely to be the salary payable to a five-year or more qualified senior solicitor or salaried partner.

It used to be the case that the general rule of thumb for profitability comprised one-third of fees allocated to salary costs, one third to other overheads and one-third for the equity partners. These rather general ratios are quite out of date and most firms would be very happy if they could be achieved. The pressure on fees and expenses is much greater nowadays, and profit margins tend to be less.

Staff costs, excluding notional equity partner salaries as a percentage of fees, can vary greatly. A good ratio would be 40 per cent, but often the proportion is just more or less than 50 per cent. A proportion near or more than 55 per cent can be a warning indicator, unless there are very few equity partners in proportion to fee earners.

Staff costs including notional equity partner salaries run usually towards 60 per cent and can be higher, although if they are significantly higher, then this can be a warning sign.

A useful comparative efficiency indicator is total fees divided by fee earner costs, including notional equity partner salaries. This gives the amount of fees earned per £1 of salary costs and gives an efficiency ratio that can be used for comparison purposes. The proportion of non-fee earning staff costs can also be an indicator. This kind of analysis may, however, have to wait until more detailed information is available.

Other overheads as a percentage of fees can be an indicator of whether the firm's overhead base is too great for its size. Premises costs can be influential in that a firm that has been in an old office for many years can benefit from very low premises expenses, which can distort the ratio. It is usual to separate premises expenses (rent, rates, heating and lighting, building insurance, repairs and renewals, etc.) from other overheads. If premises costs exceed 10 per cent of fees, this can be an indicator that they are expensive, or if they are significantly lower, it can indicate they are very low. If the business operates from a freehold property a notional rent should be imputed, although mortgage interest would, in turn, be excluded from calculations. Overheads other than premises expenses should generally be carefully considered if they exceed 20 per cent of fees.

Equity partner profits, both in absolute terms and as a percentage of fees, are absolute and proportionate comparators. Various benchmarks are available, but comparisons between the firms and against expectations are probably the most significant. One of the objectives of a merger should be to at least maintain, if not improve, equity partner profits.

Equity profit, both in absolute terms and as a percentage of fees after equity partner salaries, indicates equity investment return, albeit that these indicators are not based on capital invested.

The total of capital and current accounts equates to the net assets in the balance sheet of the respective firms. This can be an indicator of financial stability: too low a figure can indicate poor profitability or overdrawing, whereas too high a figure can indicate poor credit control with too high a debtor level, or a large amount of capital tied up in fixed assets, or simply undrawn cash.

The level of work in progress in the accounts is of interest. Again, the difference between the firms can be significant, and also the absolute level or percentage of fees, as this can throw up valuation differences or other issues.

Bank indebtedness is always of critical interest. Current levels should be considered, together with the reasons for any high levels of indebtedness. There may be good reasons, but this is an area that can be critical in merger discussions, as it can either indicate a philosophical difference in the way the business is run or highlight other issues.

Timetabling

As with any project it is essential to have a plan or budget; in this case, a timetable. An initial timetable should be established either at the end of the first meeting (if successful) or no later than the beginning of the second meeting.

Unless exceptional reasons exist for rushing the process, realistic timetables should be established to provide adequate time for full due diligence and consideration of all issues. Any attempt by one party to hurry things should be regarded with circumspection by the other party.

A two-stage approach to a merger is usually optimal. There should first be an agreement in principle to merge following satisfactory pre-merger enquiries. Heads of terms should be engrossed in an agreement to merge. Following the signing of the agreement, a detailed implementation schedule should be established and a firm date set for the merger to take effect.

It is possible that phase one of the process, involving due diligence and the negotiation of the agreement to merge, could take up to three months depending on the size of the firms and the complexity of the issues involved.

Phase two of the process could take a further three to six months, again depending on the size of the firms and the complexity of the issues. Nevertheless, once a merger has been agreed, there are many issues concerning the operation of the new firm that need to be very carefully planned and thought through in detail. If hurried or glossed over they could lead to a difficult situation a year or two later. The main issues at stake comprise the financial arrangements and detailed administrative systems of the merged firm, the management structure for the new business, the handling of staff issues, premises issues and IT systems. The success or failure of a merger will revolve as much around the goodwill and support of employees as the involvement and support of partners.

Taskforces

Following the first meeting and establishment of a timetable, whether or not a facilitator is involved, it is essential that at least one partner and one member of the administrative staff, preferably the practice manager or equivalent, are appointed as the merger planning team or steering group. Each firm's steering group will tend to operate in conjunction with, but at some distance from each other, but should also act as one team once the agreement to merge is signed, on the basis of having joint responsibility.

The issues to be tackled need to be divided up into the various aspects: financial, legal, premises, IT, resources, personnel, PR and any other areas that are considered important.

It is possible that sub-committees will be needed if the merger is between sufficiently large firms, with external advisers being involved in their specialist areas, for example, external accountants on the financial side and the IT managers on the IT side. However, it is essential that an overview is retained by the responsible partner(s) and appointed administrative staff member. In smaller mergers, they may handle all aspects with external advisers as often the practice manager is directly responsible for the financial, premises and IT aspects of the practice.

It is essential that the taskforces' terms of reference are agreed and specified, and timetables set and adhered to. In phase one, leading up to the agreement to merge, their tasks will be to obtain information and identify issues that will need to be resolved, and to determine that they can be resolved. The individual taskforces will report back to their own firms, through the main steering personnel.

When all the issues have been considered 'back at base', the contentious areas need to be identified and agreed internally by each firm, and a position achieved that covers what would be acceptable as a resolution for each matter. Each firm should then exchange details of the issues that each has, and a joint negotiating meeting should be arranged to resolve them. The meeting should be recorded and involve the decision-makers of each firm, who should have a mandate to bind their respective firms.

Once an agreement to merge is signed, the implementation timetable should be set and the taskforces reviewed. It is essential that their thrust is changed from one of enquiry and gathering of information to one of cooperation and problem solving.

Information gathering is generally initiated by a questionnaire.

External advisers

It is essential that external advisers are used strategically and effectively. They should not be allowed to drive the process. They should be requested to provide information as instructed. This is where a project manager or facilitator who has been through a merger and/or has been a professional adviser can help.

Often, when no independent person is available, the firm will turn to accountants for assistance. It is essential that the person involved has experience with a merger or can call on someone who does. If this experience is not available, it is usually advisable to seek specialist help from someone familiar with the merger process and requirements.

These comments are made for two main reasons: to control costs and ensure, as far as possible, that external advisers do not interfere with or sour the process due to over-zealousness or partiality. They should be instructed that it is not their role to negotiate, which should be left to the principals.

Communication

Ideally, there should be no communication outside the partners and selected administrative staff until the agreement to merge is signed. This is often difficult because word can leak out. Hopefully, this will be confined to employees, and it has to be handled based on the circumstances that arise. Employees usually know when something is going on, although they often do not know that a merger is in prospect. Invariably, the partners say that the process is part of a business review or budget process.

It is important that no impression is given that there may be a merger before an agreement to merge is signed. This can often result in the process falling apart for a number of reasons, including chagrin at the disruption and embarrassment caused at the other firm. It is, therefore, important to keep an ear to the ground, and it can assist if meetings are held after normal working hours and/or offsite, albeit that internal meetings should not be too much of a problem. Common sense has to prevail.

Once an agreement to merge is signed, it is essential that communication is handled in the right way, including the order that people find out, which should be employees first, clients second and the outside world afterward.

A meeting of all employees, or series of meetings held very close together, should be arranged immediately after the agreement to merge has been signed. Ideally, a formal presentation, providing information and assurances on what will be happening, would be made. This presentation should be planned and coordinated with the merger partner to ensure that the message is consistent. When employees are away from the office, they should ideally be notified by telephone or letter so that the chances of finding out about the merger from elsewhere are minimised.

Virtually at the same time, letters and emails should go to clients announcing the merger and the benefits that it will provide. No standard letter exists, as each merger is different, but it is essential to be clear and positive about what will happen. Give assurances on standards of service and personnel, as well as fee levels.

Once employees and clients have been informed, it is usual to write to key contacts (mainly banking and other professional contacts) and suppliers, as well as release a press statement announcing the intention to merge and a broad timetable. Again, the positive aspects of the merger should be emphasised, particularly the benefits to the firms and clients.

Further guidance on mergers

This chapter was first published in the LMS Legal Aid Toolkit. Further guidance on mergers is available in the LMS mergers toolkit.

Case study

Mid-tier commercial firm in major regional city

How many partners does your firm have?	12
How many fee earners (including partners, paralegals and trainees) does your firm have?	50
What is your position in the firm?	Managing partner
Who is responsible for financial management?	Board member
Could you indicate what action your firm has had to take so far in dealing with the recession?	Increased bank borrowing to fund redundancy costs. Reduced payroll by 15 per cent. Reduced operating costs by 5 per cent. Upped business development efforts in areas where we are doing well. Used opportunity to clear dead wood. Introduced Equitrac to recover copy costs.
Do you have any particular suggestions as to things that have worked in helping your firm adjust?	Act decisively. Staff understand the climate and know things have to be done. Communicate constantly with stakeholders especially banks.
Were there any ideas that have not worked?	No
Do you have any suggestions for managing debtors and WIP?	Measure cash collection at individual, department and firm levels. Communicate with debtors effectively and be creative. Avoid a blanket policy of stat demands.
Do you have any suggestions for engaging partners and fee earners and getting them take action to reduce the amounts tied up in working capital?	Provide information in a form they want/ understand.
What are the main problem areas you face in making progress?	Getting the lawyers to understand the real world.
What are the main figures you now look at each month to monitor the financial health of the business?	Daily/monthly cash collection, billing versus cash collection.
For how long do you expect the current recession to last, specifically in terms of the legal sector rather than the economy at large?	Activity will be slow for at least two more years. A lot of firms won't survive. Those that do will be those with sound finance, niche players, those strong in the right sectors or good at snaffling market share.
Who in your firm is responsible for managing:	
(a) utilisation and fee earner payroll costs;	(a) Managing partner/board
(b) leverage and secretarial to fee earner and support staff to fee earner ratios;	(b) Ops manager
(c) support staff payroll costs;	(c) Ops manager
(d) non-payroll overheads.	(d) Ops manager
Any other tips?	Keep positive. Do the financial hygiene. Innovate in business development (which doesn't just mean following the obvious commoditisation route although some will find that an answer – and good luck to them).

Chapter 11

Tackling change positively

Fiona Westwood[1]

It is important that your firm is ready for the upturn. To achieve this, it is essential to build your firm's confidence in managing change in a positive and constructive way. Few people are comfortable with the uncertainty caused by the current economic climate, so it is essential therefore to identify a number of practical projects that bring positive benefits to everyone.

Knowing what you are good at and doing it well

For any business to be successful, it needs to know what it is good at and to do it well. For a professional firm, this means that it needs to ask its clients why they chose the firm to provide a service for them over its competitors and more importantly, why they continue to use it. I am afraid that I am not an advocate of sending out pro forma client questionnaires on completion of a piece of work. At best, it will achieve a limited response and at worst, it will annoy some clients who will feel that, not only has the firm charged them for every minute of its time but now it expects them to gift some of their time to it by completing a feedback form. In my experience, firms will achieve much more of value by speaking directly to some targeted clients, even going to see commercial clients in their place of business. It is important to ask them what went particularly well for them and what they felt could be improved.

Given current pressures to reduce operational costs, it is essential that you carry out this exercise as soon as possible before decisions are made that may fundamentally damage your 'unique selling proposition' (to use some marketing speak). This investment of your time will provide a lot of useful information about what aspects of your service your clients really value and where you can focus your efforts when working for them in the future.

Such questions will produce a lot of important information about:

- what went well and why the client thought that;
- what could be improved and why;
- areas where the client felt that too much information was provided;
- areas where there was too little information;
- tone and preferred type of communication;
- time delays that could have been avoided;
- information they would have liked in advance; and
- what other support could have been provided to them.

1 Fiona Westwood is a former solicitor and now consultant with Westwood Associates and a founder member of the Law Consultancy Network.

All of this is extremely useful and will help to inform your decisions about how to reduce operational costs, what services to expand and skills to develop. If you are currently making such choices without this information from clients, you risk undermining the very part of your firm that clients feel make it successful.

Having identified what you are good at, you must ensure that you continue to do it well. It is essential that actions to reduce your cost base do not damage the firm's ability to maintain its service consistency and quality. If, for example, you close a branch office and clients are forced to travel a distance to deal with an unfamiliar receptionist and new professional, they may feel a drop in quality of care and attention. You also need to be careful about how clients and the market perceive changes that you make, especially ones that are obvious to them. Closing a branch office may appear to the partners to be no more than a sensible decision to reduce operational costs. However, if that office had a considerable visible presence, its closure without adequate explanation may be read as indicating that your firm is in difficulty.

To manage change positively it is important to concentrate only on changing those aspects of your service that clients have told you that they do not consider essential to their choice of using your firm. For example, it is important to routinise those parts of handling a piece of work that the client does not actually see, such as using IT to create standard letters to other lawyers. Letters to clients should not become 'impersonal'. If there is repetitive information that needs to be given to clients, then this can become an attractive 'brochure' rather then a dull pro forma document. With every change you make, it is important to find ways to improve clients' service experience, rather than cut service levels.

Identifying and implementing internal opportunities

Earlier chapters have covered the importance of carrying out a financial audit and analysing margins and pricing. It is also important to look at all of your resources to ensure that they are being used to their maximum to deliver a consistent quality of client service. I would suggest that you consider how improvements can be made in:

- how work is being carried out;
- how time is spent;
- the risks associated with some types of work; and
- the risks associated with some types of clients.

Before the downturn there may have been work practices that you felt were inefficient but did not have the time to tackle. You now have the opportunity to do this, especially if they will result in reductions in operational costs. For example, you may always have intended to develop some underused software package to improve your workflow and/or reduce the cost base of certain types of work. Combining this with the information you have gained from your client discussions will allow you to look at the detail of how time is spent on different types of work. Your focus should always be to identify areas where time is being 'wasted', i.e. not valued or appreciated by clients so as to reduce the cost of doing the work without damaging their perception of quality.

This may also be the opportunity to move away from charging by the hour to charging for what we achieve. I have always advocated a move towards finding out what clients value, then delivering and charging for it. If we continue to charge by the hour, then clients will continue to focus on how much time we spend on a file rather than what we achieve for them. If you are an experienced and skilled professional whose firm has invested in technology and support staff to allow the work to be done quickly and effectively, even charging an enhanced hourly rate does not reflect all of that investment. For example, it may now be only taking you an hour to do what used to take you eight hours. So if you now charge £220 an hour instead of your old rate of £120, you will be paid £220 instead of £960. However, a rival firm may delegate this type of work to a less experienced assistant with an hourly charge-out rate of £160, who takes four hours to do it therefore charging £640. If you move to charging the client a set fee of £600 this is still a good price from the client's perspective compared to the competition and a much better profit margin for you.

In addition, most clients want some indication at the outset how much this matter will cost them rather than be quoted an hourly rate which gives them no useful information about what the overall cost is likely to be. Moving to fixed fees will therefore improve their perception of a quality service.

This review of work practices and time spent provides the chance to realign people's roles and responsibilities and raise the issue of succession. Some people may feel that the downturn is the chance, at long last, to work less hard and achieve more of a work/life balance or even make an exit from professional practice. It is important not to assume that everyone feels the current situation is negative and it is also important not to ignore what I describe as distress flares. Some of your partners may be exhibiting signs of wanting your attention. Some for example, may be saying 'I don't feel that I have the energy to tackle fundamental changes'. Some may be behaving in a childish way and storming about complaining about small problems. Change provokes uncertainty and induces stress and people react to stress in different ways. Managing partners must speak with all their partners on a one-to-one basis to find out how they are and what they would like to do in the longer term. Some may well be happy to retire and leave their clients and profits for younger people to take on.

This restructuring will provide opportunities to stop and consider who does what in the firm. It offers the chance to scope out people's individual strengths and identify the potential to encourage people to work together more effectively.

There may have been areas of work where the firm has been 'overtrading', resulting in client dissatisfaction or even complaints and claims. Taking the time now to set up project teams to investigate these areas will pay dividends in the future and should lead to changes and improvements in work practices, as well as a reduction in problems and fire fighting.

It is always worthwhile analysing the risks related to different types of work and clients and making changes to allow such risks to be managed better. For example, there are some types of work that rank highly in percentages of claims and complaints. The vexed area of letters of undertaking and statutory time limits continue to frustrate professional indemnity insurers who constantly ask the legal market to improve their claims record in these basic areas. Complaints also show a depressing trend of historical similarity with no real change to the underlying themes of failure to communicate effectively with clients and time delays. Now is the opportunity to set up procedures to prevent all of this. There are sectors of clients and business that are statistically higher risk areas such as matrimonial and commercial property and therefore merit special attention in terms of risk management.

Finally, in respect of internal opportunities, if people have some time on their hands, it is the chance to put together a group of people who are good at lateral thinking to identify new services. Some hints about these will have come from the client interviews, some suggestions can be obtained from business contacts and brainstorming sessions can provide a source of some innovative ideas. All of these can be turned into pilot products that can be developed and tried out.

Tackling change in a positive way creates an atmosphere of acceptance of change so that people begin to see it as something 'normal' rather than something to fear. That in turn makes people more adaptable, creating more flexibility across the firm. Implementation of change is crucial and in my experience often difficult for professional partnerships in particular with so many 'chiefs' having an opinion about what is happening in the firm. Overcoming people's reluctance to change is not easy, particularly in the current economic situation where everyone is worried – about their own and family jobs, pensions or mortgages. We will now move on to consider morale and motivation.

Managing morale and motivation

Some firms may have experienced such a reduction in work levels that staff adjustments have been required with some branch offices closed, people made redundant and/or asked to work part time. Some partners may also have decided to retire from the firm or may have been asked to do so.

Quite apart from the depressing effect on morale in the firm whilst this was happening, such changes will continue to have an impact on the people who have 'survived', with former colleagues being missed, work responsibilities having to be adjusted and clients understandably anxious about what this means for them.

It is important that all of the partners in the firm shoulder the responsibility to ensure that there is a positive atmosphere in the office as this is not something that can just be left to the managing partner and senior management team. It is also essential to ensure that there is regular and open communication to staff. It is more than likely that increased financial pressures will lead to a need for more formal partners' meetings. If staff see partners sitting for hours behind closed doors, in the absence of direct information, they may well suppose sinister reasons for this.

Even with redundancies and office closures, some people may not have enough work to do. This offers the risk of idle hands making mischief, so it is doubly valuable to turn some of the internal opportunities described above into practical and real projects with a defined timescale for completion. This will help people to feel busy and valued, particularly when so much emphasis on performance in the past has been placed on chargeable hours.

People may have to be asked to take on additional or even new responsibilities, yet people will not be willing to try to learn new skills unless they feel 'safe'. Asking people to learn, adapt and change, even at the best of times causes stress and as a result, requires significant investment in providing reassurance and support. In addition, it is important not to allow people who behave badly to get away with it. If there are individuals who are muttering against the changes needed, they must be persuaded that this is not helpful and will not improve the situation. If they have genuine concerns, these should be addressed. If they are being negative because they have a personal issue this must also be identified.

Employers sometime argue that if people are being paid to be in the office from 9.00am to 5.00pm five days a week, this is immutable or alternatively if people cannot be fully occupied, they should reduce their paid hours and take the resultant drop in salary. This does not have a positive effect on motivation and my experience of the recession in the early 1990s proves that people expand work to fill the space available. Therefore, if firms reward staff by letting them finish early one afternoon a week, they would find that people got through exactly the same amount of work as they would do if they were there the full five days. And this approach will have a very positive effect on morale.

Building client loyalty

As discussed before, clients are likely to have noticed changes especially if offices have been closed and/or members of staff whom they usually deal with have left. This will have unsettled them and, coupled with marketplace gossip about what is happening to the firm, may well be making them question whether the firm has a long-term future. It is important to provide your clients and business contacts with as much information as possible about your current and future plans. Most firms have websites and they can be very useful to get such messages across to a wide spectrum of people. Current clients who have seen a change of personnel will require more direct reassurance that their business will continue to be handled well by experienced staff who know all about their background and requirements. This brings us back round to ensuring that the 'surviving' staff sound positive and willing – not resentful and tired as can be the case when people feel put upon as result of additional workloads.

It is essential to show that firms appreciate that clients are as anxious about the future as they are. Business clients are under considerable pressure and private clients are worried about their savings, pensions, homes and work. I know that some firms have been proactive sending out bulletins to offer some guidance about market conditions, investment options and the like. Over and above that, discussed in the first section, it is always worthwhile to go and see clients personally. Quite apart from the opportunity that this presents to find out their particular concerns and identify any new pieces of work, it shows them that they are important and builds loyalty for the future. It is also the chance to explain the range of services that the firm provides. In my experience, clients continue to be unaware of the range of services provided, only seeing what is done for them at that particular time – that constant refrain of cross-selling that appears in most firms' business plans yet so rarely happens in practice. For example, you may be doing company restructuring for them, but they do not appreciate that the litigation department does employment work. The firm may be helping them with a house sale, yet they do not know that you also do probate.

Client retention and empathy with clients during turbulent economic times are important. Although business development budgets are often the first to be scaled back in any cost-cutting exercise, what really matters here is effective marketing. Having a coffee with a client may well be just as effective as more elaborate client entertaining or hospitality.

Doing more pro-bono work may seen a ludicrous idea when the firm is not getting in enough fees and having problems with cash flow, yet if people are not fully occupied, some staff may enjoy the opportunity that pro-bono work offers. It allows them to develop their skills at the same time as do something worthwhile in the community or in a particular client area, such as debt or family advice. It also shows that the firm is compassionate and committed to helping people – values that most lawyers will identify with.

Conclusion

This chapter focuses on taking the positive out of the current business climate and the changes that law firms are facing

It is important to know what your firm is good at and do it as effectively as possible. It is essential to find out from your clients what is important to them and what they are prepared to pay for. You must ensure that any changes made to the way that you operate maintain and preferably enhance service delivery.

Involving people in practical projects helps with their morale and motivation by keeping them busy and feeling that they are doing something worthwhile. This is the opportunity many have been waiting for to make significant improvements in the way legal work is carried out, reducing the time wasting elements of it and improving how we spend our time. Investing spare time now will pay long-term dividends as people become more flexible and adaptable and comfortable with change.

Case study

Top 200 portfolio law firm

How many partners does your firm have?	17
How many fee earners (including partners, paralegals and trainees) does your firm have?	55
What is your position in the firm?	Managing director
Who is responsible for financial management?	Finance director
Could you indicate what action your firm has had to take so far in dealing with the recession?	Two rounds of redundancies; activating a break-clause to release excess office space; drilling into every item on the expenditure budget.
Do you have any particular suggestions as to things that have worked in helping your firm adjust?	We had to take fairly radical action. We started the financial year 2007–08 with a fee income target of £7.3 million, providing a profit for 9 equity partners. By the time of the financial year 2008–09 we had to start with a fee income target of £6.3 million and still provide a reasonable level of profit for 9 equity partners plus keep control of the cash. No mean task!
Were there any ideas that have not worked?	Not particularly.
Do you have any suggestions for managing debtors and WIP?	We are moving to a monthly system of billing WIP. As ever, change is painful and it's an arm wrestle at the moment! We have an excellent credit controller who chases our debtors. When the clients plead poverty, the fee earners scream that they're going to lose a client. A nice balancing act!
Do you have any suggestions for engaging partners and fee earners and getting them take action to reduce the amounts tied up in working capital?	I have tried education; much closer management of WIP with team leaders making them accountable; we are now changing our terms of engagement letters and introducing a monthly billing system. The fear of the overdraft exceeding its limit seems to be the main motivating factor for the worst culprits.
What are the main problem areas you face in making progress?	As ever, driving through change is slow and a struggle.
What are the main figures you now look at each month to monitor the financial health of the business?	In addition to how much work we've made over the previous month and forecasts for the following two months we concentrate quite heavily on bar graphs showing the volume, estimated value and source of work coming in across the firm. Fortunately all graphs are in the upwards trend.
For how long do you expect the current recession to last, specifically in terms of the legal sector rather than the economy at large?	Probably Spring 2010.
Who in your firm is responsible for managing:	
(a) utilisation and fee earner payroll costs;	(a) Managing director, finance director and team leaders
(b) leverage and secretarial to fee earner and support staff to fee earner ratios;	(b) As above
(c) support staff payroll costs;	(c) Finance department
(d) non-payroll overheads.	(d) Finance department

Any other tips?	Have a good sense of humour! Being a law firm leader in this climate is a very challenging task. Not only do you have to implement extremely difficult decisions involving human beings, you have to fight and struggle in order to get the partners to accept that difficult decisions have to be faced. The amount of energy this requires is quite staggering.

Chapter 12

Conclusion

The underlying theme of this book is that firms should adopt a twofold strategy:

- The first stage is to secure your firm's financial position, in particular with regard to cash and working capital.
- Having regained financial control the second stage is to start planning for the upturn, positioning your firm so that it will survive and hopefully prosper in the even more competitive world into which firms will emerge.

The future was already going to be difficult for many firms as a result of the Legal Services Act – and then came the recession. Ironically, some firms that were well prepared for the Act have found themselves vulnerable in the recession due to their over-dependence on property. Others that were less advanced in their thinking have experienced the fall in volumes they feared as a result of the Act, and have been forced to take action that may well prove to have made them more viable in the longer term.

As Nigel Haddon says in his Foreword: 'While surviving the recession is a goal in itself, well-led firms are also planning for a return to prosperity.' You need to ensure your firm is one of them.